BUBBLEGUM
The History Of Plastic Pop

1950s
1960s
1970s
1980s
1990s....

Unknown country singer Bill Haley ditched his stetson and cowboy boots to become a rock 'n' roll pioneer

1

rock 'n' roll is here to stay

1950s

Ricky Nelson

At one stage in the 1950s, Ricky Nelson was as big as – if not bigger than –
Elvis Presley in terms of popularity, record sales and money.
But then he had his mom and pop to help him.

Ozzie Nelson was a former jazz musician turned family entertainer who, in
the early 1950s, made the transition from radio to TV with his wife Harriet,
with a hugely popular weekly show. Ricky, along with his older brother David,
had been regulars in the show until – in an eerie foreshadowing of David
Cassidy in *The Partridge Family* in the 1970s – Ricky was launched into an
unexpected, yet dynamite career as a teen pop star.

It's claimed that his first single, a 1957 cover of Fats Domino's 'I'm
Walking', was recorded in order to impress his first girlfriend. Frequent plugs
on his parents' show ensured that it stormed to Number 4 in the charts and a
well-timed move from middle-of-the-road to rock 'n' roll shortly afterwards kept
the momentum rolling.

Despite the fact that he had very little musical experience, Nelson possessed the x-factor of youth, energy and good looks in abundance. He also
had his dad's contacts book with which to recruit any number of ace session
musicians and producers. As a result, Nelson pumped out a succession of
smooth-sounding rockabilly hits which gained him more than 30 Top 40 entries
from 1957 to 1962.

On his 21st birthday in 1961, Nelson changed his name from Ricky to the
more sober Rick, but, although he continued to release his trademark upbeat
singles, he found himself – like so many of his 1950s teen idol counterparts
– elbowed out of the charts by the growing number of beat groups. Nelson
did himself few favours by trying to compete with them, when all his dwindling
fanbase wanted was to see him sing his old favourites.

In the 1970s and 1980s he spent much of his time touring. Indeed, it was
while travelling to a gig in Dallas in 1985 that he was killed, when his plane
caught fire and crashed.

The men behind the Comets were songwriter Jimmy Myers and producer Milt Gabler. Together with Haley, they set about creating a new sound and a new look which was different from anything that had been heard or seen before – especially performed by a white artist. Gabler, a veteran artists and repertoire (A&R) man turned record producer, had been responsible for the innovative jump-blues of R&B artist Louis Jordan in the 1940s, and he confessed he used much of this style when crafting the sound for Bill Haley and The Comets. 'All the tricks I used with Jordan I used with Haley,' he said. 'The only difference was the way we did the rhythm. On Jordan, we used a perfectly balanced rhythm section from the Swing era… but Bill had the heavy backbeat.'

More important than the sound, though, was the audience at which it was pitched. Prior to the 1950s, the record-buying public consisted almost exclusively of adults. Now, encouraged by a raft of radio disc jockeys prepared to play hitherto taboo rhythm and blues tracks – taboo, because in white-bread middle-class America rhythm and blues meant black music – it was the kids who were suddenly taking an interest. Instead of having to listen to Mom's Al Martino and Hank Williams records, here at least was a style of music that they could call their own. In cities across America, the local record shop soon began to rival the drive-in and the malt shop as a place where teenagers could congregate. Records like 'Sixty Minute Man' by black vocal group The Dominoes began to appear in the upper reaches of the charts.

The Comets were the inevitable consequence of this. Middle American outrage that kids were listening to 'nigger music' had done nothing to dent sales, a fact not lost on the record companies. But if the teen market was there to be exploited, far better that it was done on the record companies' terms.

It was time for white men to play black music.

Presenters, Promoters And Svengalis

While the kids lapped up Haley and The Comets, the unprecedented success of the venture inevitably attracted the interest of entrepreneurs who suddenly identified a new and vibrant marketplace. Chief among them was Colonel Tom Parker, a cigar-chomping carnival huckster from Tennessee whose only prior knowledge of the music business had been briefly managing ageing country star Hank 'The Yodelling Ranger' Snow. It was while touring with Snow in 1955 that Parker heard a raw youngster called Elvis Presley and, aware of the ruckus that Haley was creating – and desperate for his own slice of the pie – he became the teenager's manager.

Fabian

Legend has it that when talent scouts first discovered Fabian Bonaparte Forte in 1957, the 14-year-old was sitting on the porch of his house in Philadephia, weeping about the future of his impoverished Italian-American family. They saw he had the looks and the desire to make it as a pop star, and the rest is history.

Like the rest of Fabian's career, there is little doubt that its most humble and heartbreaking of beginnings was thickly embellished with showbiz gloss.

The talent scouts concerned were Bob Marucci and Peter DeAngelis, a pair of seasoned record producers, managers and songwriters who had recently revived their fortunes by signing teen idol Frankie Avalon to their Chancellor Records stable.

It was Avalon himself who pointed them in the direction of his neighbour Fabian, and in the space of just a few months Marucci and DeAngelis had transformed the gawky youngster into a heart-throb. They dressed him in V-neck sweaters to accentuate his angular features, swept his hair into an improbable quiff, and hid his acne beneath layers of make-up. They even employed a singing coach to try to improve the youngster's flat voice – although they also ensured that Fabian did virtually no live singing and, if possible, no singing at all out of the studio.

His first single, 'I'm In Love', was promoted by a series of personal appearances on Dick Clark's influential *American Bandstand* show, in which the youngster merely stood around looking moody while his record played in the background.

At first, it seemed the public weren't about to be fooled. 'I'm In Love' and its follow-up 'Lily Lou' bombed in the charts. It was only after Fabian was allowed to lip-synch to his third single 'I'm A Man' that interest was registered in the record stores.

Encouraged by this, Marucci and DeAngelis decided on a change of tack. Now that he was 16, they decided the time had come for Fabian to ditch his little-boy-lost routine and become a little dangerous instead. Unashamedly aping early Elvis, Fabian was transformed into a leering, hip-swinging predator on stage, and suggestive singles like 'Turn Me Loose' and 'Tiger' hit the Top 10.

Astonishingly, in 1959 a poll voted him the country's Most Promising Vocalist. Predictably, his pop career was effectively over by the end of the year. He was named in the American Congress as a dupe of the 'payola' scandal, in which record companies bribed radio stations to play their records. At the same time, it was revealed that the Most Promising Vocalist relied heavily on studio wizardry to improve his natural whine.

For the naive teenager, the ensuing criticism was devastating. 'It was a killer,' he said. 'It embarrassed me. I still think I have some remnants of it in my being, in my tissues somewhere. I really don't give a shit now, but mainly my sole purpose was to see if I could help my family out, which I did. Some of it was justified criticism, but a lot of the personal cruel attacks were not.'

The hits dried up and for the next decade Fabian eked out an existence by appearing in dozens of forgettable movies. An attempted comeback in the 1970s failed, and he was even reduced to appearing nude in Playgirl. His personal life disintegrated and he spent much of the intervening years in therapy. However the 1980s saw an upturn in his fortune as he began appearing regularly on a Dick Clark 1950s revival roadshow – ironically, alongside his old neighbour from Philly, Frankie Avalon.

The story of Parker's Svengali-like influence over Presley from those early days until the singer's death in 1977 has been well documented. Theirs was also a unique arrangement. Whereas entrepreneurs turned managers like the UK's Larry Parnes had a stable of starlets who were created, paraded and quickly ditched Elvis Presley was Parker's one and only act.

'Elvis has required every minute of my time,' Parker said, 'and I think he would have suffered had I signed anyone else.'

At the same time, Presley himself was possessed of a unique talent which, until his own demons caught up with him, was able to withstand not only Parker's machinations (the movie career doldrums of the 1960s and the Vegas treadmill of the 1970s), but the fickle fashions of pop music. Presley spent more than 20 years at the top, while the average shelf life of contemporaries such as Fabian, Frankie Avalon and Rick Nelson was little more than 18 months. 'The King' was manufactured all right – but only in the way the highest-quality diamond is cut and shaped from the rough.

No matter how photogenic the artist or astute the manager, bubblegum pop could not exist without the oxygen of publicity. In the days before MTV and wall-to-wall music radio, there were two ways an act could hope to succeed in tapping the hearts and pocket money of the vast youth market: by getting their record played on the handful of national radio shows which actually acknowledged rock 'n' roll or, even more crucially, securing a slot on *American Bandstand*. In this respect, the two men who did most to boost the careers of America's teen idols were Alan Freed and Dick Clark.

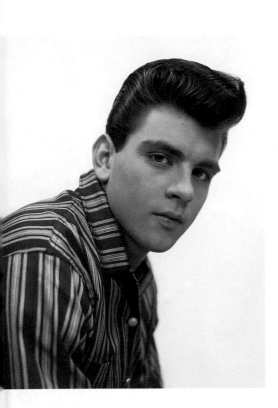

Fabian: utterly talentless, he was banned from singing his own records live on TV

Col Tom Parker: carnival huckster who became the manager of rock 'n' roll's greatest star

Alan Freed was one of the architects, if not the architect of rock 'n' roll's popularity in the 1950s. Indeed he is often credited with having invented the term. A DJ from the backwaters of Ohio, Freed set out to popularise his beloved rhythm and blues music among a white teenage audience.

'Good music is good music, no matter who plays it,' Freed said. 'What's important is that people are able to hear it in order to make up their own minds.'

Such was his success that in 1952 he staged a concert of predominantly black R&B acts in Cleveland, which attracted 10,000 fans and 6,000 gate-crashers. Significantly, more than two-thirds of the audience was white. Two years later, Freed's radio show transferred to New York, where it swiftly became number one in the ratings. Live shows featuring new rock 'n' roll acts were a huge success, and Freed himself starred in the bandwagon-jumping movies *Don't Knock The Rock*, *Rock Around The Clock*, and *Rock, Rock, Rock*.

But, like many of the acts he promoted, Freed's moment in the spotlight was to be fleeting. In 1957 ABC-TV gave Freed his own nationally televised rock 'n' roll show, but an episode during which the black singer Frankie Lymon danced with a white girl enraged ABC's southern affiliates and the show was cancelled. At the same time, the authorities – who already had Freed at the top of their hit list – began clamping down on his live shows. A disturbance at one show in Boston in 1958 led to Freed being hauled up on charges of incitement

Credited with inventing the term 'rock 'n' roll', DJ Alan Freed died destitute after the payola scandal

Frankie Lymon and The Teenagers

'Oh no, I'm not a juvenile delinquent!' sang fresh-faced, 14-year-old Frankie Lymon in 1956.

Unfortunately, he was – and, after a further decade of heavy drinking, smoking cigars and substance abuse, Lymon was found dead on his bathroom floor with a syringe sticking out of his arm. He was 25.

It is unclear whether Lymon's meteoric rise to fame or post-pubertal failure conspired with heroin to kill him so young. The answer is probably a mixture of the two. Barely in his teens, he had become America's first black singing idol and, with his group The Teenagers (average age 16), the inspiration behind every black vocal group from the Jackson 5 to The Drifters. Indeed the group's distinctive sound and routines would provide the blueprint for the Motown era of the 1960s.

They had fallen under the wing of influential New York record-company boss George Goldner as early as 1954, but it was not until 1956 that The Teenagers made their breakthrough. The song was 'Why Do Fools Fall In Love' and, as usual, it was immediately covered by a respectable white group, The Diamonds, who were fully expected to take it to the top. The difference this time was that the kids went crazy for Lymon's version. The Diamonds were consigned to the dustbin of history and The Teenagers were made.

Sporting a clean cut image so as not to offend middle-class white American parents, the group were choreographed by the great Cholly Atkins (who would later go on to greater fame with The Temptations), wore V-necked sweaters, and had their hair brilliantined so that, on the monochrome TV sets of the time, it was quite possible to imagine that they were, in fact, white.

In just a few short months in 1956, Lymon and The Teenagers had appeared with The Platters and Bill Haley, hit the charts with a second single, appeared on the top CBS TV show *Shower Of Stars*, toured with 'The Biggest Rock and Roll Show of 1956', and begun production of a movie. By the end of the year, they had released five top-selling singles and an album.

If it all appears now to have been an unseemly rush, then it was with good reason. The following year, Lymon's voice broke. Without his distinctive soprano to lead, the group never recovered. Two subsequent singles bombed, and in the summer of 1957 Lymon quit. By 1958, he was a heroin addict. He entered a drug rehab programme in Manhattan in 1961, but couldn't remain clean.

In 1966, arrested on yet another heroin charge, Lymon entered the army in lieu of a jail sentence but was soon kicked out with a dishonourable discharge. He married three times, but was never able to settle down. He was found dead on the bathroom floor of his grandmother's New York apartment, where just a few years earlier he had enjoyed a happy and, for a while, anonymous childhood.

'I'm not a juvenile delinquent,' sang Frankie Lymon (second from right). Sadly he was – and he would be dead within a decade

to riot, which in turn led to the cancellation of his New York radio show. In 1959, his career was effectively ended by the payola scandal in which he was named as one of the prime beneficiaries of the money-for-air-time scam. He died in 1965 aged just 43, broken and destitute.

Another prominent music celebrity summoned to testify in the payola scandal was Dick Clark. It is testament to Clark's popularity and influence in 1959 that he was exonerated completely. Alan Freed, for all his enthusiasm, had never captured the imagination of the teen audiences, or succeeded in overcoming the suspicion of the authorities. He was already in his mid-30s at the height of his fame, with a face that looked ten years older. During his live shows, he had the unfortunate habit of dancing awkwardly on stage – beside artists often half his age, he looked embarrassingly like their square dad.

Clark, on the other hand, had the clean-cut looks and all-American charm that rock'n'roll so desperately neededa if it was to be accepted by a wider television audience. He also possessed a shrewd business-man's brain and an instinctive knowledge of the youth market.

While working as a DJ in Philadelphia, Clark was chosen as the presenter of a local TV music show called *Bandstand* in 1956. The format

Payola

By the mid-1950s, independent record companies had broken the stranglehold of the majors on airplay, and their songs dominated the charts.

The response of the majors, in the shape of the ASCAP (American Society of Composers, Authors and Publishers) was to accuse the independents of paying DJs to play their records. This was a practice which had been going on as long as the music business itself, but with the subsequent payola investigation, ASCAP – which had always regarded rock 'n' roll as a passing fad – would try to bury it for good.

Fearing the worst, the independents began stepping forward and announcing that they had given money to specific DJs. Soon 25 DJs and programme directors were caught in the scandal, including the two biggest – Alan Freed and Dick Clark. Clark, with more to lose, quickly gave up all his musical interests when ordered to do so by ABC-TV.

The fall guy for the whole payola scandal was Freed. When asked to sign a statement denying involvement, Freed refused – and was promptly fired from his job with New York radio station WINS.

was simple and rigid: an invited audience of clean-cut teenagers would be invited to dance along to middle-of-the-road offerings from the charts. Clark, then aged 26, was no teenager – but he had an uncanny knack of interacting with his audience on their own level. He quickly realised that *Bandstand* was hardly representative of what was really going on in the real world.

In 1957, the show, renamed *American Bandstand*, went national. With the clout of network exposure behind him, Clark began to remould the show. Instead of dreary recordings, the latest new acts – particularly the new rock 'n' rollers – were invited to perform live (or, rather, mime live). This development immediately made *American Bandstand* a magnet for record promoters, as a slot on the show would guarantee thousands of sales the following week. Just as in the UK the pop show *Oh Boy!* offered a platform for Marty Wilde and Billy Fury, artists like Fabian, Paul Anka, Bobby Rydell and Frankie Avalon owed their early success directly to their exposure on *American Bandstand*.

It also gave Clark unparalleled power within the industry. He had shares in several of the major new record companies and partial copyright on 150 songs, many of which were played on the show. As Hank Ballard of The Midnighters admitted, 'The man was big. He was the biggest thing in America at that time. He was bigger than the President!'

Now firmly established in the US, there was only one way for the new teen revolution to go – and that was across the Atlantic. Trouble was, the only link that Britain had with rock 'n' roll was the fact that Bill Haley's mother had been born in Ulverston in Cumbria.

But change was in the air – and, with it, the untold riches of a fresh and vibrant marketplace. All it needed was someone to tap it. That man was Larry Parnes.

Parnes, Shillings And Pence: The UK's Home-grown Teen Idols

The first show Larry Parnes organised featured an all-singing, all-dancing cast of child performers. It was a big hit, especially for Parnes, who pocketed over two shillings in box-office receipts. In those days, that was big money for an eight-year-old.

Within 20 years, virtually the same formula had earned Parnes millions and created a stable of teenage pop stars that would cement his position as the first and perhaps greatest svengali in the history of British popular music. It was Parnes who took gawky teenagers such as Ron Wycherley, Reg Smith, Clive Powell and Tommy Hicks and, at a stroke, turned them into Billy Fury, Marty Wilde, Georgie Fame and

Tommy Steele: the cruise-liner cabin boy who became the UK's first rock star

Tommy Steele, dashing heart-throbs with knock-'em-dead names. It was Parnes who told them what to wear, what to say and what to sing. It was Parnes who milked them for all they were worth on gruelling roadshow tours the length and breadth of the country. And it was Parnes who dumped them when they outlived their usefulness.

Thirty years before Stock, Aitken and Waterman's stable of overnight sensations dominated the charts, and almost half a century before the lucrative teen market was targeted by TV shows like *Popstars*, *Pop Idol* and *Fame Academy*, Larry Parnes was churning out chart-topping rock 'n 'rollers to order.

Of course, Parnes was fortunate inasmuch as he arrived on the music scene at the very moment it was undergoing a seismic revolution. In America, the rough three-minute rock of Elvis Presley and Bill Haley was causing a sensation in a nation more accustomed to Mantovani and Frank Sinatra. The rule book was being ripped to shreds along with cinema seats. When Haley arrived in the UK by train in 1957, there was a near riot at Waterloo Station as thousands fought to get a glimpse of their man. His subsequent 45-minute gig at the

Tommy Steele

Unlikely as it may seem, Tommy Steele – the cheeky, chirpy Cockney perhaps best known for his tombstone teeth and his version of 'Little White Bull' – was, for a few short months in 1957, Britain's answer to Elvis Presley.

That he was, owes more to the considerable skills of his marketing and management team of John Kennedy and Larry Parnes than to the inherent musical appeal of Steele himself. Indeed Steele's brand of rock 'n' roll was decidedly bland compared to the raw and revolutionary sound that Presley was blasting out from across the Atlantic. At the same time as Steele released a foot-tapping version of Guy Mitchell's 'Singing The Blues', for example, Presley was recording the seminal 'All Shook Up'.

Steele himself freely admits that he was never much of a rocker. 'Larry used to ring me up with names: "What do you think of 'Marty Wilde' or 'Billy Fury'?" "Yeah, that sounds nice." And, to be honest, they were far more committed than I was. I was really a country singer who was emphasising the second and fourth beat. I never went looking for screams and gyrating and quivering my bottom lip. Because of that, I was like the answer to Elvis! In Sweden they had a poll to find out who was the best rock 'n' roller – and believe it or not, I beat Elvis!'

But what Steele lacked in rockin' pedigree, he more than made up for in good old-fashioned personality. His was a 'working-class boy made good' story that, when expertly polished by Parnes and Kennedy, captured the imagination of the British press and public alike.

He was born Thomas Hicks in 1936 in Bermondsey and, living in London's Docklands, it was no surprise that he found his first employment as a seaman, both in the merchant navy and, more glamorously, as a cabin boy on ocean liners.

Young Tommy's first love was music, however. Whenever he could, he would escape to the skiffle clubs of the capital's West End, where he loved performing solo with his guitar.

It was while performing in the 2is Coffee Bar – a venue that also hosted unknowns such as Terry Nelhams and Harry Webb, who later became Adam Faith and Cliff Richard – that he was first spotted by Lionel Bart.

Bart was blown away by Tommy's self-assurance and by his dazzling good looks. In 1956, along with Mike Pratt, they formed a group called The Cavemen that began performing the circuit.

Tommy Steele

However, it was not until Bart asked his friends John Kennedy and Larry Parnes to take a look at the group that Tommy's career took off. In typical style, Parnes immediately changed Tommy's name from Hicks to the more dynamic Steele, and sent him for an audition with his old pal Hugh Mendl at Decca.

'He sang "Rock With The Caveman",' Mendl recalled. 'I knew nothing about what he would sound like on microphone, but to me there was a fabulous magic. Everybody was being rude about rock 'n' roll but this was such a magical performance by a magical performer. Two days later we had him in the studio performing his first record.'

Meanwhile, the Parnes–Kennedy management axis was cranking itself into a frenzy. Kennedy delivered a masterstroke when he booked the Cockney-born Steele to perform in front of hundreds of high-class young girls at a debutantes' ball. The 'Debs' Delight', as Steele was christened by the press, was suddenly a star. 'Rock With The Caveman' climbed into the Top 20, Tommy was making regular appearances on *Oh Boy!* and Parnes was telling everyone who would listen that he had unearthed 'Britain's answer to Elvis'.

'The kids weren't fooled,' argues former Wham! manager Simon Napier-Bell. 'They knew Tommy was no match for Elvis Presley – his sex appeal was nothing more than a sweet dumb grin. But they didn't care. They didn't love Tommy Steele because he was sexy, they loved him because he'd managed to do something never before done in the British music business. Be young!'

What was in no doubt was that Tommy Steele was the first British pop star. And, as such, he would provide the blueprint for the archetypal career in bubblegum pop: shine as brightly as a magnesium flare, then fade away just as quickly.

In Steele's case, the glory days lasted little more than a year. After reaching number one in January 1957 with 'Singing The Blues', he went on to have four songs in the Top 30. At one stage, he was provoking the same sort of teen hysteria that characterised the concerts of American star Johnny Ray.

But, by 1958, Parnes had turned his attention – and that of the audience – towards his growing stable of teenage stars, many of whom, such as Marty Wilde, were young enough to make even 21-year-old Tommy look geriatric.

For his own part, Steele was shrewd enough to realise that it was time to diversify. After appearing in the movie *The Tommy Steele Story* in 1957, he moved into a moderately successful film career. By the end of the 1950s, he had all but abandoned rock'n'roll for a career as a family entertainer. The release of the novelty record 'Little White Bull' in 1959 was a statement of intent as much as it was a farewell to pop stardom.

For some, Tommy Steele was never anything more than a novelty act. Guitarist Brian Gregg says, 'Tommy was supposed to be our answer to Elvis, but he quickly became a George Formby character and nobody took him seriously as a rock'n'roll singer.'

Dominion ended with the police wading into swaths of hysterical kids stampeding after his limousine.

Parnes watched the developing scene with a shrewd eye – and four things struck him immediately about the rock 'n' roll phenomenon.

First, the records were being snapped up by kids.

Second, the kids were less interested in raw talent than they were in image. Most of the time, their screaming meant they couldn't even hear the artist on stage. Presley's sneer, Gene Vincent's blue cap – even the overweight Haley's kiss curl – were gimmicks that were hugely effective and marketable.

Third, the potential market was huge and untapped. Quite simply, there was no pop industry in Britain in the early 1950s. The biggest stars were bland crooners such as Dickie Valentine, David Whitfield, Frank Ifield and Ronnie Carroll. The hottest group were The Inkspots, who sang racy numbers like 'Whispering Grass'.

But what impressed Parnes most of all was the totalitarian manner in which the artists were controlled by their management. Despite being the biggest star in the world, nothing that Elvis Presley either said or did was not first sanctioned by Colonel Tom Parker. The temperamental Gene Vincent was skilfully puppeteered by the vast A&R department at Capitol Records. Frankie Avalon was told to sing in a high, nasal voice.

Parnes moulded his artists accordingly. 'I have their hair cut – that is very important,' he explained. 'Sometimes they may have bad skin which has to be attended to. Then I get them suitable clothes and provide them with comfort. I like them to have a touch of luxury from the start.'

Parnes also exerted total editorial control over his protégés. Marty Wilde, who was just 16 when Parnes signed him up in 1957, recalled: 'Larry got me a public relations officer, people looking after me, a bodyguard. One always had to be very careful what one said to the press. I was never really allowed to say what I really thought. When I did I was either shot down in flames by the press or by Larry when I got back.'

And that was not all. Parnes, a voracious homosexual, enjoyed surrounding himself with young boys – especially those who were desperate for their shot at the big time. According to former Wham! manager Simon Napier-Bell, Parnes' London flat was '… always full of boys who come to see him hoping to be chosen. If Larry likes the look of them, he gives them a clean white T-shirt and tells them to hang around. If a boy's wearing a black T-shirt, it means Larry's had him already and his friends can have a go if they want to.'

Elmer Twitch? You must Be Joking!

Larry Parnes was born in 1930 in the unspectacular London suburb of Willesden, with the equally unpromising showbiz pedigree of an uncle who performed in pre-war music halls under the name of Len Young the Singing Fool.

Marty Wilde

1955 had been a good year for the Philips recording company, with middle-of-the-road artists such as Doris Day, Johnny Ray, Ann Shelton and Frankie Vaughan providing them with an unprecedented 26 weeks at Number 1. Now, they decided, it was time to see if the Midas touch would work in the so-far untested waters of the youth market – and this was to prove the making of young Reg Smith from London.

Reg, like most teenage wannabes hoping to follow in the footsteps of Tommy Steele, was performing with a skiffle group at clubs like the 2is and the Condor, banging out the standards and keeping one eye out for Larry Parnes. He had even changed his name – to Patterson.

In the event, it was Lionel Bart who discovered him. Bart had been asked to go talent-spotting by Philips' A&R department, and one night in the Condor Club he realised that he might have found his boy.

The 16-year-old Reg was dispatched to Parnes, who liked what he saw. The only thing he didn't like was Reg Patterson. Out came the coin [see BILLY FURY], and two spins later Marty Wilde was born.

'Knowing Larry, it was probably a two-headed coin,' Wilde said later. 'Once I'd been going for three months and got used to it, I realised what a great stage name it was. It is one of the best names I've seen in print. If you're trying to sell tickets, it just looks good – I can't explain it, but it does.'

But, while he was initially happy to leave his name, image and public relations in the hands of his new manager, Wilde was determined that his lasting reputation would be for his singing voice.

'[Parnes] could not train me as a singer,' he said. 'In the end he never even tried.

Sometimes he would try to show you a movement and then we'd all break up in hysterics.'

Similarly, Wilde never took himself too seriously. While Terry Dene fervently believed he could challenge the might of the Americans, Wilde was simply content to enjoy the ride while doing a professional job. He enjoyed the adulation of teen crowds, but was never seduced by it into thinking he was anything other than an entertainer.

Perhaps because of this reticence to play pop star, his early singles bombed. But Parnes stuck by him and ensured that he received plenty of television exposure. He became almost a resident performer on *Six-Five Special*, where his vocal ability was often in stark contrast to the three-minute tyros who appeared with him. Eventually he began to grow on audiences, who appreciated that here was a rock 'n' roll artist who might just amount to more than a quiff and a snarl.

In 1958, the time and effort paid off and Wilde reached No 4 with 'Endless Love'. His *annus mirabilis*, however, was the following year when, as well as four Top 10 singles – including the enduring 'Teenager In Love' – he secured regular top billing on Jack Good's new show *Oh Boy!*

Yet, no sooner had he gained the high ground than Wilde lost it. Good, wary of allowing *Oh Boy!* to become stale, already had his eye on a new young performer called Cliff Richard, whose début single 'Move It' was being touted as a genuine rival to the rock 'n' roll coming out of the States. Parnes, unwilling to have his boy playing second fiddle to another performer, pulled Wilde from the show.

While that move may seem in retrospect to have pulled the plug on Wilde's career, in truth he was already looking at the wider picture.

Mild-mannered Marty Wilde eventually reached the top – although he never believed his own hype

Perhaps reluctant to compromise his vocal expertise, he concentrated instead on reinventing himself as a crooner, producing lavishly crafted cover versions of US songs.

As if to cement the move into respectability, he married former Vernons Girl Joyce Baker, and began hosting a TV show called *Boy Meets Girl*. Although a version of Bobby Vee's 'Rubber Ball' brought him belated Top 10 success in 1961, Wilde's career as a rocker was effectively dead and buried. Subsequent singles failed to trouble the charts, while a group formed with Joyce and Justin Hayward, later of the Moody Blues, made no impression.

Wilde, though, seemed blissfully unconcerned. Indeed, he was happy to have been a part of the nascent British pop industry without ever becoming a sad old has-been. He retained a strong fanbase that saw him comfortably through the 1960s, and in the 1970s and early 1980s he was proud to have been a part of his daughter Kim's chart success. Today he tours regularly, his distinctive voice as strong as ever.

Billy Fury

Inevitably, it was Parnes who gave Billy Fury his stage name. The manner in which he did so says much about the hold he had over his young protégés. 'My name was still Ronnie Wycherley and I was trying to come up with a good stage name,' Fury recalled shortly before his death in 1983. 'I had one: Stean Wade, which came from the days when I liked country and western music. I had a call from Larry Parnes saying I had an interview with the *Daily Mirror*, because I had my first record out called "Maybe Tomorrow". Before going to see the Mirror, Larry asked me what I thought about having a stage name. I said I was fine about it. "What do you think of Billy Fury?" he asked. Well I liked Billy, because I had an Uncle Billy – but I wasn't too keen on the Fury. Anyway, we tossed a coin and I won the toss. The next day there was a picture of me in the paper and I was expecting it to say Stean Wade. Instead, it had Billy Fury!'

Their paths had crossed in 1958, when 18-year-old Billy sent Parnes a demo tape including four Elvis covers and one self-penned number. Parnes was suitably impressed and summoned him to the Essoldo Theatre, across the Mersey in Birkenhead, where Marty Wilde was headlining a Parnes roadshow.

Armed only with his guitar, Billy performed two impromptu numbers in Wilde's dressing room. Parnes was as blown away by the youngster's looks and talent as he had been by Tommy Steele's two years earlier. He signed him on the spot and then dispatched him on stage, where he brought the house down.

With his new name, and with Parnes's magic touch to guide him, Billy's career took off almost immediately. Although his early singles – generally up-tempo rockers, many of which he wrote himself – tended to hang around outside the Top 10, Parnes ensured that his boy did not go unnoticed. By the end of 1959, Billy had already made his debut as an actor in the ATV play *Strictly For Sparrows* (a bit part in which he plugged his new single), and was a regular on the top-rated TV pop shows *Cool For Cats* and *Oh Boy!*

Meanwhile, he was living in the house that Parnes had provided for his growing stable of young stars. It was here that he developed a penchant for industrial quantities of marijuana. As his girlfriend Lee – who would later marry DJ Kenny Everett – recalled, 'A lot of them smoked grass and did pills, thousands of them. Billy smoked grass from when he got up in the morning to when he went to bed at night.'

Although he knew it would ruin the squeaky-clean image of his boys were their drug consumption ever to go public, Parnes tolerated it because soft drugs were a lot easier to disguise than hard drink. And, in any case, the likes of Billy Fury attracted nothing but positive press.

At the turn of the 1960s, Parnes decided it was time for a change of emphasis for his star performer. Instead of rock 'n' roll, Billy turned to ballads – and it was to prove an inspired switch in musical styles. His version of Tony Orlando's 'Halfway To Paradise' stormed the charts in 1961 and was followed in rapid succession by hits such as 'Jealousy', 'Last Night Was Made For Love', and 'It's Only Make-Believe'.

By the mid-1960s, however, even the innovative Billy Fury was regarded as old hat. His career stalled and defied various attempts to kick-start it back to life – although this was less to do with his talent than his growing ill health. In 1971, he endured open-heart surgery, although this did not prevent him from appearing in a triumphant Wembley Stadium show alongside Little Richard, Jerry Lee Lewis, Bill Haley and Bo Diddley a year later. In 1973, he even sent himself up in the movie *That'll Be The Day*, playing a camp ballroom singer called Stormy Tempest.

In 1982, however, Billy collapsed with kidney failure and was paralysed down one side. The following year, while recording a comeback album, he fell into a coma from which he never recovered.

There are those who blame Larry Parnes for Billy's early death. His brother Albert Wycherley said, 'Larry Parnes knew all along that Billy was unhealthy, but that didn't stop him working him six nights a week and maybe sending him off to do a one-night concert on the Sunday.'

But these were claims that Parnes always denied. 'I didn't work Billy hard. We didn't discover until 1962 that he had any form of heart trouble at all. I would never overwork anyone with a heart defect. I am the last person to do that.'

Terry Dene

Terry Dene was the nearly-man of the early British rock scene, a singer whose burning belief in his own abilities was disastrously undermined by both circumstance and reality.

In 1956, he was plain old Terry Williams from London, working as a record packer by day and performing in clubs at night. Yet, even as he handled records by Elvis and Bill Haley, he simmered with resentment that these megastars were earning millions while he, who surely had more talent, languished in anonymity. In particular, he saw little difference between himself and Presley, and longed for the big break that would prove him right.

It came in 1957, when Jack Good, producer of *Oh Boy!*, happened to be at a wrestling match where Terry was singing between bouts. Good passed him on to his old friend Larry Parnes, and the renamed Terry Dene set off on the now-familiar path of single releases and TV appearances.

Unfortunately, Parnes's stardust never seemed to land on Dene. His first three singles all went into the Top 20, yet incredibly all were scuppered by rival renditions. Dene's version of 'A White Sports Coat' reached Number 18 while the King Brothers got to Number 6, 'Start Movin'' would have got higher than Number 15 had Sal Mineo's version not got to Number 16, while – most galling of all – Michael Holliday's version of 'Stairway of Love' reached the heady heights of Number 3 while Dene's languished at Number 16.

While it was not failure by any means (Billy Fury took more than two years to get his first Top 10 Hit), Dene took it badly. In 1958, he was fined twice in three months, first for drunk and disorderly behaviour, and second for vandalism.

'Okay, I was walking down the street in my underpants, but it was blown up out of all proportion,' Dene explained. 'These days it would be looked upon as a joke, you'd be some kind of streaker. But because I'd done that and thrown a No Waiting sign through a window, it caused a sensation.'

At first, Larry Parnes was secretly pleased at the screaming headlines that Dene was generating. But it was becoming abundantly clear that the mental state of his young charge was plummeting irreversibly. Dene was conscripted for National Service in 1959, but discharged after only two weeks on medical grounds.

'It was brought up in Parliament and everyone was wondering why they had taken "Screwball" in the first place,' said Dene. 'I knew before I went in the forces that there was an element of risk. I'd a long record of being medically unfit, but, because I was a big success, a lot of that was pushed under the surface. When things did go wrong, they went wrong in a very short space of time.'

This time, Parnes decided Dene was becoming a liability and that it was time to cast him adrift. Dene's threatened nervous breakdown followed soon after.

After years in the wilderness, Dene made an unexpected comeback in the 1970s as an evangelist gospel singer. Ironically, his iconoclastic and troubled personality made him a perfect role model for the punk movement, and in 1978 Decca released a compilation album of his singles entitled *I Thought Terry Dene Was Dead*.

Terry Dene thought he was the new Elvis, but pressed the self-destruct button instead

'He had quite a few publicity people around you, protecting you every time you had an interview,' recalled Marty Wilde. 'You were advised where to go for your suits and your haircuts and everything else. Although there was a slight amount of discipline involved, I would say Larry was the best manager this country ever had.'

Parnes was in no doubt as to his own ability to spot a winner. 'Tommy [Steele] was a great, great talent,' he recalled. 'He was the first one in his field, and I felt I should try someone else, to see whether I'd really got talent for producing and promoting these people. Then came Marty Wilde, totally different to Tommy in every way. When Marty hit the top and had hit records, I thought, "Well, I'm still not sure. I'd better try again", and this is how this so-called stable of stars came about.'

2

Monkee-ing around? Not likely. Davy Jones and the boys were part of a carefully calculated pop phenomenon, the first band created specifically for TV

time for some monkee business

1960s

The term 'manufactured pop' is often seen as one of abuse. Here-today-gone-tomorrow artists ridiculed as fluff. Their managers and promoters vilified as sharp-suited sharks out to make a quick buck. Yet it is worth remembering that by the end of the 1950s the concept of 'pop' was barely five years old, and in that in that short time the monster had grown exponentially, fuelled by a seemingly unquenchable energy and innovation, and by a unique ability to reinvent itself at the drop of a hat. It was a creature which simply did not – could not – allow itself to stand still for a moment.

Could this have happened without the bubblegum popsters and their Svengalis on both sides of the Atlantic? Absolutely not. 'Pop' is, after all, short for 'popular' – and popularity is a fleeting thing. This is why even the superstars of the 1950s music scene – artists and managers whose meteoric success must have convinced them they were invulnerable – would become distant memories within a few short months of the start of the 1960s.

But if the new decade brought musical sophistication and artistic longevity with bands like The Beatles, The Beach Boys and The Rolling Stones, it did not spell the end of manufactured pop. Far from it. Pop's core audience – the kids – was as voracious and fickle as ever. They still wanted new idols to pin on their bedroom walls every week. The challenge for the music industry was to find new ways in which to keep them satisfied.

The New Generation

In the early 1960s, pop music found itself in a curious state of role reversal. A decade earlier, America had been rocking while Britain slumbered in a state of chronic musical lethargy. Now, thanks largely to the success of The Beatles and The Rolling Stones, it was America that seemed comatose while across the pond the UK was suddenly a hotbed of innovation and musical creativity. A new generation of musical sophistication had arrived: all across the country, kids who had been inspired by the rock 'n' roll revolution of the 1950s to pick up a guitar – kids like Eric Clapton, Keith Richards, Ray Davies, John Lennon and Paul McCartney – were forming bands with like-minded youngsters and creating their own music. And, while most professed to have been influenced by the likes of Billy Fury and Marty Wilde, the Larry Parnes era already seemed like a distant memory.

Manufactured pop was not dead, however. Not by a long chalk. While managers and record producers in the 1960s knew it was no longer a case of selecting a good-looking boy, changing his name, giving him a song and sitting back to watch the royalties roll in, they also knew that Parnes's underlying business principles still held strong.

When Brian Epstein first saw The Beatles on stage at the Cavern Club in Liverpool in 1961, he saw four scruffy teenagers who swore a lot, smoked and drank like troopers, and played a ragged mixture of original material and clapped-out 1950s standards. Epstein, who ran

the family electrical business at the time, became their manager. He knew little about the workings of music business, but he was a consummate businessman who understood Parnes's credo that image – at least initially – was more important in getting a band noticed in a crowded marketplace than talent. Talent, if it existed at all, would come later. The Beatles were transformed overnight: the leather jackets were replaced by smart lounge suits, swearing and eating on stage was banned, and a repertoire was rehearsed until it was note-perfect.

In London, meanwhile, the equally astute Andrew Loog Oldham was busy transforming a group of polite, middle-class R&B enthusiasts into the archetypal bad boys of rock. When it came to the direction Oldham wanted for the Rolling Stones, his philosophy was simple.

'History provided the obvious agenda,' he recalled. 'Elvis versus Pat Boone, Cliff versus Billy Fury, Bing versus Frank Sinatra, Diana Dors versus Hayley Mills…Even in the 1980s it was Madonna versus Gloria Estefan, the slut who slept her way to the top versus the Cuban housewife. It's always the trash versus good boys window of opportunity in which youth gets to tell its parents who it wants to become and identify with by its musical and visual choices.'

Trash versus good boys? Stones versus The Beatles? Commercially, it couldn't have worked out better if Epstein and Oldham had sat down and planned their musical assault on the 1960s together. The incendiary conflict of 'good versus bad', carefully stage-managed by promoters and fought out in the charts, has been at the heart of pop music ever since.

The Money Machine

It is hugely ironic, not to mention extraordinary, that even as Epstein was creating a musical phenomenon in The Beatles he had already signed a deal which denied the band millions of pounds in merchandise loot. 'It was Epstein's one big fuck-up,' said John Fenton. And he should know: Fenton was one of six young business associates of Epstein who purchased The Beatles' merchandising rights for a staggeringly minuscule 2 per cent. They themselves awarded themselves 20 per cent of the retail, which in just six months netted them over $7 million. An indication of how massive The Beatles were is the fact that Fenton and his cronies sold over three million mop-top wigs in Japan alone.

Merchandising would, understandably, become the *raison d'être* of many of the bubblegum bands that followed over the next 40 years. Although The Beatles can never be accused of cashing in on negligible musical talent, in the early years especially the band generated far more wealth through their merchandise than through record sales.

Even here, Epstein had struck an amazingly bad deal. The producer George Martin, who had signed the group to EMI and would be instrumental in shaping their unique sound, had done so for a penny

Brian Epstein transformed the Beatles from Scally scruffs into mop-top megastars, but died at the very height of their fame in the 1960s

Herman's Hermits

In 1963, The Heartbeats were just like any other aspiring but uninspiring Manchester pub band, chugging their way through the standards and hoping one day to be like the Beatles.

Their luck changed the night Harvey Lisberg and Charlie Silverman happened to see them. The two young entrepreneurs were looking for a vehicle for 16 year-old former child actor Peter Noone, and The Heartbeats looked to be just what they were after.

The band, now with its fresh-faced lead singer installed, and renamed Herman's Hermits (allegedly because of Noone's uncanny resemblance to the cartoon character Sherman from *Bullwinkle And Rocky*), became an instant hit in the clubs of the northwest and soon began to attract the attention of the London studios.

In 1964 they were introduced to producer Mickie Most, who decided to sign the band to the Columbia label, largely on the strength of what he thought was Noone's uncanny resemblance to John F Kennedy. That same year, 'I'm Into Something Good', an unnervingly bouncy version of Earl Jean's US hit, shot straight to Number 1.

There it might have ended, had it not been for an extraordinary surge of popularity in the USA, which saw them score 11 Top 10 hits in two years. This success was due largely to the band cashing in on America's love affair with anything British. With the heart-throb Noone up front, they evolved a quintessentially English cheeky-chappie act playing vaudevillian boots-and-braces songs such as 'Mrs Brown You've Got A Lovely Daughter' and 'I'm Henry VIII, I Am'.

Tellingly, these songs were never released in the UK. Instead, the Hermits turned to experienced writers like Graham Gouldman (later of 10cc) to provide them with more conventional songs such as 'A Must To Avoid' and 'No Milk Today'.

'We made very good records for teenage girls,' Noone later admitted, 'Herman's Hermits was a band for teenage girls. We made records about love and romance. We were all nice chaps and they knew it.'

Inevitably the infatuation quickly wore thin and the hits dried up. In 1970 Noone left the band to pursue a solo career, although the Hermits have since occasionally reunited for oldies tours.

per double-sided single. Martin gave the band a four-year contract, increasing by just a farthing a year if he decided to renew it.

But it is perhaps too easy to criticise Epstein for his naivety. With The Beatles, he was taking the role of pop manager to previously uncharted waters, dealing with global markets that had never before been tapped. Suddenly music was walking hand in hand with merchandising. And, having been badly stung by his early deals, Epstein quickly wised up. After the first few months, he refused to authorise any new merchandise, leaving John Fenton and his colleagues with no money to pay an enormous tax bill. A deal was struck in which The Beatles paid Fenton's tax liability in return for their rights.

Epstein, meanwhile, was now busy creating his own stable of Liverpool-based artists. Rightly, he calculated that the success of The Beatles would be bound to rub off on other Merseyside artists – and he would not make the same mistakes that he had with the Fab Four. Sure enough, the likes of Gerry and The Pacemakers, The Big Three, Billy J Kramer and The Dakotas, The Fourmost and Cilla Black netted his stable nine Number 1s in 1963 alone, and made Epstein a very wealthy man by the time of his untimely death four years later.

He's into something good: thanks to cute singer Peter Noone, Herman's Hermits were huge stars on both sides of the Atlantic

Cilla Black

Priscilla White was a 19-year-old cloakroom attendant at the Cavern Club in Liverpool who occasionally moonlighted as a guest singer on quiet nights. With her strident voice and larger-than-life personality, she soon attracted the attention of Brian Epstein who, in 1963, signed her up to his growing stable of Merseyside acts.

For her first single, Epstein shrewdly handed the newly renamed Cilla Black an unused Lennon and McCartney single, 'Love Of The Loved', which did the trick of launching her into the UK Top 40. It was not until producer George Martin came on board that Cilla's career really began to take off, however. In 1964 she released the Burt Bacharach-penned 'Anyone Who Had A Heart'. This was to be the first of many brassy, overblown orchestral ballads that, in the space of just a few months, made her one of the country's top-selling artists.

Not everyone was convinced of her talent, however. Simon Napier-Bell memorably described Cilla as having a 'huge wailing voice with which she desecrated American hits made by Dionne Warwick, the subtlest singer in pop'.

Still, this seemed to matter little to Cilla's fans, and even less to Cilla herself, who never made the mistake of taking herself too seriously. By the mid-1960s, and now astutely managed by her husband Bobby Willis, she was already cashing in on her 'girl-next-door' appeal by appearing in her own TV show in which she mixed songs with wacky sketches. This served to keep her public persona at a sufficiently high level that she was able to score Top 10 hits throughout the 1960s. In the 1970s, she packed in singing altogether in favour of a burgeoning TV career which, by the mid-1980s, had made her the highest-paid family entertainer in the business.

A voice like the Mersey foghorn didn't stop cloakroom attendant Cilla Black from becoming an unlikely star, thanks to Brian Epstein's influence

Fixers And Fixes

The payola scandal in the USA had understandably made British TV companies nervous. While pop shows like *Ready Steady Go* had inherited the crown of *Six-Five Special* and *Oh Boy!* and were offering a radically different style from the squeaky-clean entertainment offered by Jack Good in the 1950s, they were equally determined not to be in the pocket of record company fixers. *Juke Box Jury*, meanwhile, was controlled totally by its host David Jacobs, who arbitrarily chose the five records to be judged a hit or a miss every week. Even then, the 'jury' tended to be made up of middle-aged celebrities whose tastes leaned heavily towards the conservative.

Fortunately for the fixers, *Ready Steady Go* and *Juke Box Jury* were not the only outlets for their artists.

Commercial 'pirate' radio was broadcast from rusting old ships moored in the North Sea and was as ramshackle an operation as it sounds. The pirates were forever being harassed by the authorities for broadcasting illegally; they frequently went off air; and the sound quality was ropey to say the least. But crucially, pirate radio's young DJs offered a trendy alternative to the stuffed shirts at the BBC, and the kids loved them for it. The fixers loved them more, however, because the pirates would quite happily accept money to play records. In fact, they were so upfront about it they introduced a sliding scale: the more money, the more the record was played.

It was a godsend, and enabled promoters and managers to buy hit singles for their bands. As a result, bands were hastily constructed for that very purpose, as enterprising young entrepreneurs clamoured for a slice of the action.

One such duo was Ken Howard and Allan Blaikley, a pair of jobbing songwriters who realised that they could make more of an impact – and more money – by combining their talent with management. Two bands they signed up in the early 1960s were The Sherabons, a workmanlike five-piece from London whose claim to fame was a female drummer, and Dave Dee and The Bostons, a group from the backwaters of Wiltshire who mixed standards with comedy routines. Under Howard and Blaikley's influence, The Sherabons became The Honeycombs and, with the help of the pirates, scored an immediate Number 1 hit with 'Have I The Right'. The cumbersomely renamed Dave Dee, Dozy, Beaky, Mick and Tich ditched the comedy and were rewarded with eight custom-made Top 10 hits including the chart-topping, whip-cracking theatrics of 'Legend Of Xanadu'.

I have a cunning plan: pictured here with The Dave Clark Five, former actor Dave Clark (laying across the car bonnet) masterminded his own rise to the top, and became a multi-millionaire at just 21

The Dave Clark Five

The Dave Clark Five remain unique in the pantheon of manufactured pop stars inasmuch as they manufactured themselves.

Or rather Dave Clark did. A former film extra, 20-year-old Clark realised that pop music could offer far more lucrative opportunities than bit-part acting. And, also aware that agents and managers tended to make a killing on the back of their clients, he decided the best way to cash in was to form a group, get a hit record, and ensure that he had signed a deal guaranteeing himself a healthy slice of the profits. Installing himself behind a drum kit (although he would always ensure the kit was installed at the front of the stage), Clark surrounded himself with a coterie of talented musicians including singer and keyboardist Mike Smith, whose vocals – when they could be heard above Clark's industrial drumming – provided the group with a distinctive edge.

What Clark could not have been expecting was the extraordinary success his Five would have. In January 1964, they released 'Glad All Over', which stormed straight to Number 1, ousting The Beatles' 'I Wanna Hold Your Hand' and, for a while at least, prompting some commentators to claim that the Fab Four had been usurped by the Cockney Five.

This was not to be, although their next single 'Bits And Pieces' reached Number 2 and, in 1965, the band starred in their own film, Catch Us If You Can. Where the Five found most success, however, was in the USA where performances on the influential Ed Sullivan Show put them at the forefront of the 1960s Britpop invasion and ensured Clark's cheeky smile was pinned up on bedroom walls across the country.

By 1967 the group's appeal had begun to pall – although Clark wasn't particularly bothered. From day one he had been on a non-negotiable 20 per cent of each record sold and was, by the age of 21, a multi-millionaire.

Hit Factories

America could be forgiven for not knowing what had hit it. At the end of the 1950s, it ruled the pop world with stars like Elvis Presley and Bill Haley. Within three years, however, Chelsea boots were walking all over it, as the British invasion – led by The Beatles and the Stones – began in earnest. Haley was old hat and even Presley was perceived as having left his best days behind him.

It was not until the mid-1960s that the US pop industry staggered back off the ropes and began to hit back. When it did, it proved that it had lost none of the innovation that had invented rock 'n' roll music a decade earlier. And it was perhaps fitting that, after seeing their rhythm and blues music purloined by white musicians, it was a predominantly black institution that took the vanguard.

Berry Gordy Jr had started Motown Records in 1958 with an $800 loan from his family and a vague notion of creating a small, independent label for unknown black singers from the ghettos of Detroit. It was when The Marvelettes landed a million-selling Number 1 with 'Please Mr Postman' in 1961 that Gordy realised he was on to a winner.

The genesis of The Marvelettes is typical of the way Gordy ran his Motown empire, and how the phenomenon of girl groups emerged in the early 1960s. The group consisted of five Michigan schoolgirls led by Gladys Horton, who were spotted at a local talent contest by Robert Bateman, one of Gordy's scouts. Gordy signed them up and immediately passed them into the hands of Bateman and songwriter/producer Barry Holland. The duo wrote 'Please Mr Postman' and installed the girls in a studio with Motown's in-house band, Earl Van Dyke and The Funk Brothers who, with bassist James Jamerson and drummer Benny Benjamin in particular, would provide the backing for almost all of Motown's artists during the 1960s.

Gordy, meanwhile, was busy perfecting an image for The Marvelettes, one that would provide the template for all of his girl groups. Motown would come to symbolise the ultimate in black musical power, but in the racist America of the early 1960s Gordy knew that black was definitely not beautiful. Subsequently, Gladys and the girls were dispatched to the hair salon, where their natural Afro style was ironed flat and teased into spectacular Middle American beehives. Powder was applied thickly to their faces so that on monochrome TV they looked white. Of course this was nothing that had not already been done in the 1950s with Frankie Lymon and The Teenagers – even down to the white-bread clothes they were given to wear – but it was to remain a distinctive Motown look even when racial tensions in the US had eased sufficiently for other black artists to express themselves more naturally.

Gordy's control of his stable of artists was total, from the clothes they wore to the songs they were given to sing. The 'Motown Sound' was an unmistakable brand and was, in the early days at least, far more important than the groups who were recruited to perform it. Gordy at

Berry Gordy (right), mastermind behind the Motown empire and the man who discovered some of the finest black artists. Pictured here with Tony Bennett, Quincy Jones, Stevie Wonder and Babyface at a LA awards ceremony in 1999

The Marvelettes, featuring lead singer Gladys Horton, were the blueprint for Berry Gordy's stable of Motown girl groups

times resembled an army general, moving his troops about wherever and whenever the front line needed bolstering. The Marvelettes underwent dozens of personnel changes in their career – even losing singer Gladys Horton in 1967 – but the idea of them disbanding was out of the question as long as they were still selling records. At one stage they were augmented by Florence Ballard of The Supremes, a band who themselves survived more than one line-up change.

Super-K

If Britain's Larry Parnes was the man who first drafted the blueprint of manufactured pop music, then it was America's Jerry Kasenetz and Jeff Katz who not only embraced the concept but enthusiastically took it to its most obvious conclusion.

Indeed it was this enterprising pair of New York record producers who first coined the term 'bubblegum' for the succession of gloopily saccharine foot-tappers that they churned out in the late 1960s. And never was the term 'one-hit wonder' more appropriate than for the stable of bands they created specially for the purpose during this time. Groups such as Ohio Express, The 1910 Fruitgum Company, The 1989 Musical Marching Zoo and Lieutenant Garcia's Magic Music Box tended to last only as long as their record was in the charts. After that, the motley collection of session musicians responsible would split up – only to reform a few weeks later as Crazy Elephant, Rock 'n' Roll Dubble Bubble Trading Card Company of Philadelphia 1914, or what-ever eye-catching name Kasenetz and Katz could dream up next.

Super-K, as they became known, had a simple strategy: to provide stripped-down, danceable pop for kids who were too young to under-stand the progressive – and psychedelic – rock scene of the time, and for adults who were too old. Musically and lyrically, the complexity of the typical Super-K record was barely above kindergarten level. Yet songs like 'Yummy, Yummy, Yummy (I Got Love In My Tummy)' and 'Simple Simon Says' would become instant and enormous global hits.

Super-K first met at the University of Arizona in the early 1960s. Apart from a love of gridiron football (Katz was on a football scholar-ship and Kasenetz was one of the coaches), the pair identified in each other an eye for the main chance. In their case, it was the music busi-ness. Although neither of them had any musical background, it struck them that here was a field in which even a lack of talent was no impediment to riches, provided you had a game plan.

The pair teamed up a few years later in New York, where they began to manage acts in Greenwich Village. One of their early clients was a group called The Palace Guards, who were subsequently signed up by Mercury Records. Super-K were so disgusted with the

Surf music was the West Coast phenomenon which produced the multi-talented Beach Boys. Oh yes – and it also produced The Surfaris

The Surfaris and Surf Music

While rock 'n' roll gave new voice to the teen generation, surf music was the first to be specifically manufactured to appeal to a particular lifestyle. In retrospect, it was the ideal choice, celebrating as it did all that was good about clean-living American kids having fun in the sun. It was rock with pearly-white teeth and a suntan.

The godfather of the surf music craze was a Californian guitarist called Dick Dale, who pioneered the genre's distinctive twanging reverb sound and, in 1961, released a single called 'Let's Go Trippin''. The record was never more than a minor West Coast hit, but it struck a chord with the small surfing fraternity, who found the sound and the sentiment a perfect accompaniment to their pastime. In the space of a few months, surf groups had spread across southern California like a rash and it wasn't long before the major record companies were sitting up and taking notice. Good-looking teenagers were snatched from the beaches, thrown into a studio with a producer and session musicians, and turned into one hit wonders like The Chantays, The Rip Chords and Ronny and The Daytonas. Surf music even flourished where there wasn't any surf: The Astronauts were from Colorado, while The Trashmen came from Minneapolis.

The Surfaris were responsible for the period's most enduring early anthem, 'Wipe Out' — although it was typical of the machinations of the industry that they had little to do with the subsequent progress of their career. On the strength of the 1963 hit, the band – a four-piece from Glendora, California – were invited to record an album. They were understandably aggrieved to discover that the music on the resulting disc had been played by a rival group, The Challengers. Things got worse the following year, when the band arrived to record their third album to discover a group of session musicians had been employed in their place. In 1965, they quit surf music for the quieter pastures of folk rock.

Had The Beach Boys not had the extraordinarily talented Brian Wilson in their ranks, they would almost certainly have gone the same way. Their early records featured session musicians, and it was only Wilson's songwriting ability that enabled them to transcend the genre and emerge as a creative force to rival The Beatles and the Stones in the mid-1960s.

resulting single release that they quit management and decided to take up producing.

From the outset, the music was always secondary to the pursuit of money. The pair developed a reputation for writing and bashing out discs in record time, and for using paid-for session musicians rather than bolshy, time-wasting artistes.

Doug Grassel, who played guitar for Ohio Express, recalls, 'They'd tell us, "Keep it simple. Hurry up. You're costing us money." They'd tell us what songs to play. And if we didn't like a particular song, they'd say something like, "Who do you think you are? Jimi Hendrix?"'

B-sides were a particular bane in their lives. After all – who listened to B-sides? Consequently, Super-K would use any old rubbish to fill up the empty space, including, on one occasion, a prerecorded song played backwards.

They may have been an abomination to the increasingly self-absorbed music world, but there was no denying Super-K's success. In 1969, at the height of their powers, they reported an 85 per cent sales increase on the previous year, recorded 25 Top 10 singles and earned a cool $25 million.

And at times it was hard not to chuckle at their sheer brass neck. In 1968, they took over New York's Carnegie Hall for a promotional concert in which their entire stable combined to form the 46-strong Kasenetz–Katz Singing Orchestral Circus. Shortly after this triumph, the duo recorded *Classical Smoke*, an album of bubblegum versions of music by Wagner, Beethoven and Mozart, as well as their own composition, *Orgy Of Lust*.

Super-K's bubblegum era would last into the early 1970s until even Kasenetz and Katz concluded that it had lost its flavour. From 1972, the duo dabbled with a succession of biker-style groups in a bid to cash in on the Led Zep/Hawkwind/Free phenomenon. But they would have to wait until 1977 before one of their groups, Ram Jam, had a hit with 'Black Betty'.

Hey Hey It's The Prefab Four

While Super-K cornered the market in cheesy insta-pop, one area they never attempted to expand into was television. As far back as the 1950s, promoters had recognised the importance of the fledgling medium and shows like *Oh Boy!* and *American Bandstand* to the success of their acts. In the 1960s, apart from the pirate stations, the gog-glebox had all but made radio redundant as a showpiece for newly created performers.

The pop video as such had yet to be invented, but in 1964 the two Beatles movies *Help!* and *A Hard Day's Night* showed the enormous potential of what could be achieved with a budget and with a lot of imagination. The following year, a couple of young TV producers did just that…and took the world of manufactured pop into a new dimension.

Madness!
Auditions!
Folk and Rock musicians/singers for acting roles in new TV series. Running parts for 4 insane boys age 17–21

So ran the now-infamous advert placed by Bob Rafelson and Bert Schneider in Variety magazine in the autumn of 1965. Its cheerful tone masked a certain degree of desperation, however. This was a last throw of the dice before their pet project was put down.

It had begun a year earlier, when both men had watched *A Hard Day's Night* at a Hollywood cinema and been blown away by its innovative freewheeling style. Here, they realised, was proof that it was possible to make a film about a pop group that was watchable and, even more amazingly, that some pop stars were actually capable of acting.

They were quickly disabused of that last notion once they started holding auditions for their own, TV-based version of *A Hard Day's Night*. The bands who turned up for screen tests, which included The Lovin' Spoonful, proved to be uniformly terrible, most of them so laid-back that they were horizontal.

'None of the groups had the "primitiveness" we were looking for,' Rafelson said diplomatically. With Columbia Pictures' Screen Gems subsidiary starting to ask awkward questions about the series they had commissioned, Rafelson and Schneider decided there was only one thing for it – create their own band.

Over 430 applicants replied to the ad in *Variety*. They included such future luminaries as Stephen Stills (of Crosby, Stills & Nash), Danny Hutton (of Three Dog Night) and Harry Nilsson. Applicants found themselves being pelted with building blocks and pieces of fruit. Rafelson and Schneider observed how they reacted, and from that determined if they had the requisite 'insanity' for the series. But whether it was primitiveness or insanity they lacked – Stills was, in fact, let down by his hair and teeth – none were in the four who were finally selected.

With his concave face, Mickey Dolenz had a natural advantage in as much as he actually looked like a monkey. A child actor in the 1950s series *Circus Boy*, he had been bumming around LA with a number of unsuccessful bands. Another actor hired by Rafelson and Schneider was British-born Davy Jones, whose claim to fame before decamping

The Crystals

For 'The Crystals' read 'Phil Spector', for it was the influential and eccentric record producer who created the identikit girl group in the early 1960s and shuffled their personnel throughout the decade to suit his requirements.

Essentially, the group was a vehicle for Spector's innovative and instantly recognisable 'Wall of Sound' production technique, which featured lavish orchestration, thumping percussion and layers of echo. It was a style that was allied closely to his own perfectionism.

La La Brooks of The Crystals recalls: 'Spector was like God. He gave me a hard time getting the takes, sometimes 20, sometimes 30 takes. Even when he had the perfect take he would say do it over.'

Spector had discovered The Crystals recording demo tapes in the Brill Building, and they fitted the bill perfectly for his vision of an all-girl group. Indeed, although The Crystals enjoyed chart success with hits including 'Da Doo Ron Ron' and 'Then He Kissed Me', they were never more than a testing ground for the techniques which Spector would perfect with The Ronettes. They were also a vehicle for some of Spector's more unusual songs. When they released 'He Hit Me (And It Felt Like A Kiss)', horrified radio bosses banned the record.

The line-up changed constantly and, although Brooks was nominally the lead singer, she never enjoyed the kudos and identity of Ronnie Bennett, the singer with The Ronettes, upon whom Spector lavished much of his time, effort and best songs. This had a great deal to do with Spector's infatuation with Ronnie, whom he later married. Once established, The Ronettes quickly superseded The Crystals in Spector's list of priorities and, after their two 1963 hits, quickly faded into obscurity.

'He Hit Me (And It Felt Like A Kiss)' was just one of the many experimental songs producer Phil Spector gave to his house band The Crystals

to the US in the mid-1960s was appearing in *Coronation Street*. The two true musicians in the 'group' were Mike Nesmith and Peter Tork, a pair of jobbing performers who had made little impression on the folk circuit during the early 1960s.

The band – Jones on vocals, Tork on bass, Dolenz on drums and Nesmith on guitar and woolly hat – were immediately placed on a strict contract in which they were paid a wage per episode. The contractual restraints would predictably come back to haunt all concerned, but for the moment everyone seemed happy.

'We are different from other groups because other groups work for themselves,' Jones explained in 1966. 'They have someone backing them who makes 25 per cent maybe, but most of them come out with 60 per cent of the profits. We don't. We work on a flat salary and no matter how much we make they give us the same salary. We renegotiate the next year for a new contract because we're sold for another year. It's like a company. We work for them. We're not being used because I'll never do anything I don't want to do. If I hadn't got along with the guys I would have left, but as it happens we all get along great together. We work well together I think.'

Transmission of the first episode was pencilled in for 12 September, 1966. For six weeks during the preceding summer, Rafelson and Schneider put their boys through the equivalent of boot camp, teaching them how to act together, improvise together, be primitive and insane together. But by far the most important skill that was drilled into The Monkees was the ability to mime. For, after an initial attempt at letting the quartet off the leash to compose and play their own music, Rafelson and Schneider realised to their horror that their recruits were no Fab Four.

It was at this point that Screen Gems decided to take a more active hand in proceedings. The Monkees would provide the vocals, but the music would be written and played for them. A musical director was required – someone who could generate the songs which would make the series a hit. It was time to send for Don Kirshner.

In the 1950s, Kirshner, whose previous claim to fame had been a failed writing partnership with Bobby Darin, had the novel idea of reviving the concept of Tin Pan Alley – the collection of music publishers on Broadway – but sticking it under one roof.

In 1958, the 24-year-old Kirshner joined forces with publisher Al Nevins to form Aldon Music. They bought premises at 1619 Broadway in New York, a run-down building otherwise known as the Brill Building. The resulting musical sweatshop would employ some of the brightest young songwriters around, who were paid $75 a day to come up with songs aimed at the burgeoning teen market. Aldon

Cartoon characters The Archies sprang from Saturday-morning kids TV to become a bubblegum phenomenon

The Archies

In many ways The Archies were the ultimate manufactured pop band. In fact they were so manufactured that they were hand-drawn. The concept was created by Don Kirshner, the musical director of The Monkees, and was simply the next logical step on the ladder: a band without the personality clashes.

The Archies started life as a high-school rock band in a comic book. In 1968, Kirshner transferred the idea to TV in the form of a Saturday-morning cartoon show. The format was virtually identical to the Monkees: a series of wacky adventures punctuated by foot-tapping songs that would then be released as singles.

Kirshner, as usual, employed a stable of established songwriters to provide the music, and an experienced session singer called Ron Dante to perform the numbers.

At first the animated group had little success, their songs deemed too saccharine and simplistic for even the least discerning record buyer. This all changed in 1969, however, when 'Sugar Sugar' became a Number one hit on both sides of the Atlantic, remaining in the top spot in Britain for a staggering four months and becoming one of the biggest-selling singles in the history of RCA Records.

All too aware of their limited life span, Kirshner milked The Archies from every conceivable commercial angle. In the US, their records appeared on the back of cereal packets and an Archies restaurant was opened in Illinois. The group even appeared 'live', when Dante and a backing band performed at a charity event in New Jersey. A second single, 'Jingle Jangle', reached the Top 10.

Kirshner, of course, was right. By the end of 1969, The Archies were yesterday's news and the kids had moved on.

Music wasn't the only publisher in and around the Brill Building. Successful songwriting teams Leiber and Stoller, Pomus and Shuman, Bacharach and David, as well as individuals like Phil Spector and Gene Pitney, could all be found plying their trade at the Brill.

But, such was the quality of Kirshner's signings, the Brill Building swiftly became a production line for some of the most enduring pop songs ever written.

Throughout the late 1950s and early 1960s, Neil Sedaka and Howard Greenfield, Gerry Goffin and Carole King, and Barry Mann and Cynthia Weill were able to churn out hits like 'Stupid Cupid', 'Take Good Care Of My Baby' and 'You've Lost That Lovin' Feeling' with almost supernatural consistency.

'Cynthia and I work in a tiny little cubicle, with just a piano and a chair, no window,' said Barry Mann in 1958. 'We go in every morning and write songs all day. In the next room Carole and Gerry are doing the same thing, with Neil in the next room after that. Sometimes when we all get to banging pianos, you can't tell who's playing what.'

In 1963, Kirshner sold Aldon Music to Columbia Pictures' Screen Gems subsidiary, of which he became president. Fabulously wealthy yet not yet 30, Kirshner soon began sniffing around for something else to occupy his time.

Two years later, he was sitting twiddling his thumbs in a meeting when the subject of two down-at-heel TV producers in Hollywood called Bob Rafelson and Bert Schneider was brought up. Things weren't going to plan with their show about a fictional, Beatles-style pop band. To Kirshner, the problems sounded like pure gold.

In June 1966, Kirchner jetted into LA with a bag full of songs written by former Brill Building employees such as Goffin and King, Mann and Weill, and his latest discoveries Tommy Boyce and Bobby Hart. (It was Boyce and Hart, a pair of failed performers, who would provide The Monkees with the majority of hits. Legend has it that they wrote 'Last Train To Clarksville', the band's gold-selling début single, during a coffee break in rehearsals.)

The series was launched in September 1966 and, after a lukewarm reception, steadily grew in popularity. Soon, over 10 million viewers were tuning in, and Monkees merchandise (in particular, replica Mike Nesmith bobble hats) was flying off the shelves. This success was replicated in singles sales. In just over 18 months, The Monkees chalked up 11 Top 40 hits and six albums that sold in excess of six million. At times, they were even outselling The Beatles.

Yet, despite this, The Monkees were always dogged by a groundswell of opinion that did not regard them as a genuine pop act – which of course they weren't. Rock critics despised them for being manufactured, and some even accused them of plagiarism. 'Such cinematic kinematics are really the property of Richard Lester [director of *A Hard Day's Night*],' said Newsweek, 'but television is a medium which thrives on thievery, and there, Beatlemania has been exchanged for Monkeeshines.'

Ironically, the people who were affected most by the manufactured pop versus musicianship debate were The Monkees themselves. Mike Nesmith in particular was becoming increasingly disillusioned and, in 1967, announced that the band were being 'passed off as something we aren't. We all play instruments, but we didn't on any of our records. Furthermore, our company doesn't want us to and won't let us.' Nesmith's comments led to a tempestuous showdown with the producers in which they threatened to suspend his contract and he put his fist through a door. Reluctant to stymie such a successful series, Screen Gems gave in and agreed to let The Monkees play their own instruments on their albums – although they insisted on releasing singles that had already been recorded by session musicians.

It was clear that the seeds of disharmony had already been sown. Don Kirshner, annoyed that his musical direction had been undermined, quit the show (a year later, he would once again be riding high with another manufactured band [see THE ARCHIES]). In 1968, The Monkees and Screen Gems were once again at each other's throats, this time over ownership of the group's name. In the end, however, it mattered little. The show's second season featured the same frenetic lunacy as the first, but audiences were beginning to tire of the same old formula. In the face of plummeting ratings, TV network NBC pulled the plug. It was September 1968, almost exactly two years to the day since the show had first aired. Just about average for a manufactured pop group.

The question of manufactured pop's legitimacy did not begin with The Monkees, but it was them – and, more particularly, their success – which brought it into focus. To the purists, The Monkees were not fit to be included in the same chart as The Beatles and The Rolling Stones, yet at their peak Dolenz and co were comfortably outselling both. Indeed, both John Lennon and Paul McCartney were fans of the show, and in particular the hits it produced. Even though they were played by session musicians, there could be no doubting the quality of pop songs like 'Daydream Believer', 'I'm A Believer' and 'Pleasant Valley Sunday'. And, of course, what the critics conveniently forgot to mention was that even ground-breaking bands like The Beach Boys and The Byrds relied heavily on session musicians on their early albums, while many of the songs on the hallowed Beatles masterpiece,

Sergeant Pepper's Lonely Hearts Club Band, were performed by Lennon or McCartney plus a coterie of their favourite musicians.

The 1960s was by no means a golden decade for bubblegum pop, overshadowed as it was by the dominance of some genuinely jaw-dropping original talent from the scrum of young bands who emerged onto the scene at the end of the 1950s. Even groups manufactured and produced by consummate hit-makers like Berry Gordy at Motown and Phil Spector have been proved by time to have been far more talented and enduring than the chart fodder spewed out in the decades that followed. Music writer Rick Kieff is one of many who believe that, 'The '60s was essentially pop music's greatest decade, a time of unprecedented creativity and originality across the spectrum.'

It is perhaps ironic, then, that when the term 'manufactured pop' is mentioned, the first band everyone thinks of is The Monkees – but even they were manufactured pop that was built to last. Everything from the songwriters to the sets had the same stamp of high-quality workmanship. If songs like 'Daydream Believer' and 'I'm A Believer' had been sung by The Beatles or The Beach Boys, no one would have lifted an eyebrow because they were that good.

But perhaps the main reason why everyone thinks so fondly about the 1960s –even aberrations like The Archies – is that they were followed by the bloated 1970s, the preening 1980s and the out-and-out commercial free-for-all of the 1990s. As the decade ended on a high – literally – with the Woodstock open-air concert, few suspected that the industry was about to dump in the pool of musical purity from a great height.

Phil Spector: filled his studio with dozens
of musicians to create his legendary Wall
Of Sound

If the 1950s belonged to the Americans and the 1960s to the British, then the 1970s saw the rest of the world – and Europe, in particular – fight for elbow room at pop's top table. This multi-culturalism perhaps explains why, in terms of musical consistency, the 1970s were such an unseemly mess. Glam rock begat stadium rock which begat disco and punk, yet the decade would end with the charts full of some of the most influential and talented artists in the history of pop. Indeed the only constant in this often dizzying whirl of styles and influences was the public's insatiable desire for manufactured pop stars.

Here, at least, the music industry did not let them down.

Take It On The Chinn: Pop To Order In The UK

In the UK of the early 1970s, the axis of pop power consisted initially of three men: songwriters Nicky Chinn and Mike Chapman, and producer Mickie Most. It was they who were responsible for churning out the majority of the country's bubblegum pop acts and, at the same time, creating a cheesy soundtrack for a generation. There are few people in their mid-30s who do not come over all misty-eyed when 'Tom Tom Turnaround' comes on the radio. Equally, it is often galling for people who proclaim the genius of The Sweet's 'Blockbuster' to discover that it came from the same collective that gave the world 'Some Girls Will' by Racey.

Nicky Chinn was a used-car salesman from London who first met Australian musician Mike Chapman in a restaurant. It was to be a fortuitous meeting. Together, Chinn and Chapman would create a musical dynasty that made them pre-eminent in the industry for the first half of the decade.

'We've probably got our formula, but if asked what it is I don't think I could pinpoint it exactly,' Chinn explained at the time. 'One of our formulas is bloody hard work! I don't think that most pop song writers, except for the James Taylors, are loaded with inspiration or anything.'

It also helped their cause that they fell into cahoots with the flamboyant Mickie Most. Their songwriting, allied with Most's production genius and industry savvy, was a match made in heaven. Most, who enjoyed travelling round London on his high-powered motorcycle, had made his name in the 1960s, first as a minor-selling artist and then predominantly as manager of The Animals. His particular forte was selecting the right song for his artists. It was Most who set Herman's Hermits on their way when he decided the relentlessly cheery 'I'm Into Something Good' would be a perfect vehicle to promote Peter Noone as a dimple-cheeked teen favourite. He was able to create hits for often the most unlikely of stars, including Lulu and Terry Reid. And it was largely down to Most's influence that Donovan, Britain's acoustic folk equivalent of Bob Dylan, switched to an electric sound for his 1966 hit 'Sunshine Superman' (although it also had a lot to do with the fact that Dylan himself had recently shocked his die-hard fans by

Session musicians could often become stars in their own right. Racey were the lucky ones on this occasion

swopping his acoustic guitar for an electric one). In 1969, after a highly successful and lucrative stint working for CBS in the States, Most returned to London to set up his own record company, RAK – and it was here that he was first introduced to the aspiring team of Chinn and Chapman.

Chinn and Chapman had already proved themselves by writing 'Lucky Lucky', a hit for The Sweet, who they were also managing. But the prolific duo had a hatful of songs in their back pocket, and it was

Producer Mickie Most was one of pop's biggest names in the 1970s, although that didn't stop him giving us Mud and Racey

to Most that they took them. One of these songs was 'Tom Tom Turnaround', which neither Chinn nor Chapman thought was among their best. Most, however, had other ideas, and gave it to the band New World, who took it into the UK Top 10 in 1971.

'He didn't seem very impressed with the songs we had played him up till then,' said Chinn. 'We had a last try with "Tom Tom" which we thought was all right, but wasn't a hit. Anyway Mickie said, "That's a hit", soon as he heard it and from that moment on we were convinced that it was a hit too.'

Armed with Chinn and Chapman's songs, Most created a succession of vehicle bands such as Racey and Mud to sing them, usually made up of whichever session musicians happened to be hanging around the RAK building in west London at the time. He was not the only one – across at Polydor, producers Wayne Bickerton and Tony Waddington were about to unleash The Rubettes on an unsuspecting public. The band was created from session singers specifically to perform the Bickerton–Waddington composition 'Sugar Baby Love' after every other group had turned it down. The song went straight to Number 1 in 1974 and for a while The Rubettes, with their trademark flat caps, were the toast of the music business.

'Fur Coats And No Knickers – And That's Just The Fellas'

The 1970s was a good decade for the purveyors of bubblegum pop, because for the first time audiences were actively demanding style over substance – and never was the concept more enthusiastically embraced than by glam-rockers. Today glam seems like a bad dream, with its weedy songs performed by long-haired blokes teetering on silver platform shoes. 'It has no substance,' said one rock critic at the time. 'It's all fur coats and no knickers – and that's just the fellas.'

Yet to dismiss it so lightly is to fail to appreciate the impact glam made in the early 1970s. After the clean-cut 1950s and 1960s, when pop singers looked like bank clerks in their smart suits and combed hair, here were artists like The Sweet, Marc Bolan, David Bowie, Gary Glitter and Slade who actually looked like pop stars. It was pure show-biz and the audiences loved it.

So did the artists. It is no coincidence that many of glam rock's biggest names were failed popsters from the 1960s who, by sprinkling themselves with glitter and giving themselves suitably outlandish names, were able to reinvent themselves and their careers. Gary Glitter, for example, had begun life as Paul Gadd, performed in 1950s skiffle group Paul Russell and The Rebels, nosedived as the solo artist Paul Raven, and was in oblivion on the club circuit in Germany when he got

The Bay City Rollers

It's tempting to think that The Bay City Rollers were an overnight success dreamed up by a marketing man, but in fact the nucleus of the group that would become the biggest teen sensations of the 1970s had been together as far back as 1965.

Back then, brothers Derek and Alan Longmuir were known as The Saxons, and they had a healthy following in the pubs and clubs of their native Edinburgh, where they toured playing cover versions of predominantly Beatles songs.

Their career defining moment happened in 1970, when they came under the wing of Tam Paton. Paton was an entrepreneur from the school of hard knocks, an intimidating man whose ambition was matched only by his desire to succeed. Paton changed the band's name to The Bay City Rollers, varied their act, and ensured that they were seen by record-company men from London. The new approach bore instant fruit when the band were signed by Dick Leahy of Bell Records and given the old Gentrys hit 'Keep On Dancing', which went straight into the Top 10 in 1971. To Paton's consternation, however, this proved to be their only hit and the Rollers were in grave danger of sinking back into the obscurity from which they had come just a few short months before.

Paton decided it was time to act. He changed the line-up once again, bringing fresh-faced Edinburgh teenagers Les McKeown, Stuart 'Woody' Wood and Eric Faulkner into the band alongside the Longmuir brothers. Deciding that the band required a gimmick, Paton brilliantly elected to play on their nationality. Thus Hibernian chic was born. From that moment on, the Rollers or their fans were never seen without bum-freezer jackets, tartan-edged ankle-freezers (trousers at half-mast), striped socks, baseball boots and tartan scarves tied around their wrists. On a more fundamental level, Paton also hired the songwriting duo of Phil Coulter and Bill Martin to generate a string of frothy, bubblegum songs that would appeal to the teenage fans he wanted to cash in on.

Coulter and Martin obliged, and in 1974 it all came together in spectacular style when 'Shang-A-Lang', 'Summerlove Sensation' and 'Remember (Sha-Na-Na)' stormed the charts and the band began to attract the kind of frenzied teen adulation not seen since the days of Beatlemania a decade earlier. Unlike Brian Epstein, however, Tam Paton kept total control of the band's merchandising deals. Not one tartan scarf or Woody wig was sold without Paton's express approval.

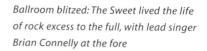

Ballroom blitzed: The Sweet lived the life of rock excess to the full, with lead singer Brian Connelly at the fore

The Sweet

One of the main beneficiaries of the glam-rock movement, and certainly the band that most people automatically associate with the period, was a pub band called Wainwright's Gentlemen, who became psychedelic rockers The Sweet Shop and then met Nicky Chinn and Mike Chapman and were transformed into The Sweet, the high priests of 1970s kitsch.

The band was fronted by Brian Connolly, who, with his distinctive long blond hair, lipstick, satin trousers and glittery platform boots, successfully disguised the fact that he was originally from a rough Glasgow tenement. Indeed Connolly's strangely androgynous look would become one of the overriding images of the glam-rock years, and was responsible for generating the band a great many more record sales than their frankly lukewarm records deserved.

Between 1971 and 1974, they pumped out a succession of Chinn–Chapman songs, the highlights being 'Blockbuster' and 'Ballroom Blitz'. Their style was a mix of campy theatrics mixed with ersatz heavy-metal thrash, and it did the trick. In just three years they sold over 50 million records. The band's cause was undoubtedly helped in 1972, when Mecca decided to ban them from their concert halls because of their 'overtly sexual stage act' and this, coupled with the band's ostentatious flaunting of their enormous wealth (Connolly bought himself a huge mansion and employed a team of staff including a butler and a maid), gave them the much-needed illusion of being real rock 'n' rollers, when in fact they were little more than conduits for Chinn and Chapman's bubblegum pop.

In 1974, foolishly believing their own publicity, The Sweet decided they no longer required Chinn and Chapman's services and released an album called *Sweet Fanny Adams* which consisted entirely of their own material. It was no surprise that the album did in the charts precisely what it said on the cover, peaking at Number 27 before slipping into oblivion. Their next album, *Desolation Row*, fared slightly better and produced the Number 2 single 'Fox On The Run', but it was obvious that their best days were behind them. In 1978, they managed a Top 10 hit with 'Love Is Like Oxygen', but it was to be their last. The band continued to pump out albums and survived the 1980s with any number of personnel changes, but the high life had caught up with the unfortunate Connolly, who in the 1990s was struck down with a muscular disorder and suffered several heart attacks. In 1997, he was felled by a fatal coronary, aged just 52.

Hit makers Mike Chapman and Nicky Chinn created some of the cheesiest – and best-loved – bubblegum chart-toppers of the '70s

'Producer Pete Shelley and I had thought of a few names and Alvin Stardust appeared,' he explained. 'We'd go through things that had influenced us in the past, like Elvis and Gene Vincent and tried to get something from that… Elvin, Alvin. We settled on Alvin. I always wore black and Pete's impression of me was that I looked like a gunslinger. Think of a name, Ringo Starr. Man In Black. Can't use Starr, so we lengthened it and Alvin Stardust was born.'

Suzy Quatro played in a Detroit garage band until Mickie Most brought her to England, dressed her in black leather and gave her a Chinn and Chapman composition called 'Can The Can' to perform. Marc Bolan had been in a late-1960s hippy acoustic band called Tyrannosaurus Rex until Kit Lambert, The Who's legendary manager, persuaded him to take electric-guitar lessons from Led Zeppelin's Jimmy Page and go shopping for women's clothes in second-hand shops on the Portobello Road in London.

'I never considered I'd be a teen idol,' Bolan said. 'I've always been into visuals. My wife had some glitter, I spit on me finger and put it under my eye. The next concert, everybody was covered in glitter.' When Bolan appeared on *Top Of The Pops* performing his chart-topper 'Hot Love' in a feather boa and with glitter on his cheekbones, shops across the country sold out of both the next day.

Starsky And Hutch *star David Soul (right)*
began his singing career as the masked
'Covered Man' on American TV

David Soul

Fans of *Starsky And Hutch* had always suspected that behind the leather-jacketed car-jumping exterior, Hutch had a feminine side he was itching to reveal. Maybe it was the blond locks that got longer with each season of the show. Maybe it was the bushy moustache that appeared without warning in series three.

Confirmation of their worst fears was provided in 1976, when Hutch got to Number 1 in the pop charts with a warbling love song entitled 'Don't Give Up On Us Baby'. Or rather David Soul did. It was difficult for fans of the show to differentiate.

Soul had been in his mid-30s when he hit the big time starring opposite Paul Michael Glaser as Detective Ken Hutchinson in the top-rated buddy-buddy cop show. But long before that he had actually started his career as a folk singer in his native Chicago. Musically, however, his career appeared to have peaked when he landed the dubious privilege of playing a masked vocalist known as The Covered Man on *The Merv Griffin Show*. Chastened, Soul concentrated on acting and might have remained a 1970s TV icon had the international fame generated by *Starsky And Hutch* not persuaded him to have one last crack at pop stardom.

Sensibly, Soul turned to an experienced producer and songwriter called Tony Macauley to provide him with what turned out to be a smash hit on both sides of the Atlantic. He would remain a one-hit wonder in the US, where he was never taken seriously as a singing star, but in Britain he scored another chart-topper with 'Silver Lady' and kept his female fans swooning with 'This Time I'm Going In With My Eyes Open'. Delighted with his belated musical success, he launched himself on a tour of the UK in order to milk it to the full.

The demise of *Starsky And Hutch* and the misfiring of his subsequent acting and singing career led Soul into a long period of drug and alcohol problems. Thankfully he is now over them and, living in London, he is an active participant in the capital's theatrical community.

Motown had done with Michael Jackson and his brothers, and in a way it harked back to the 1950s, when the pre-pubescent Frankie Lymon was catapulted to the front of The Teenagers.

But where MGM's strategy differed from Berry Gordy's was almost immediately to initiate a solo career for Donny running concurrently with his career with The Osmonds. Paeans to adolescent love such as 'Puppy Love', 'Too Young', 'Why' and 'Young Love' not only established him as the number one object of desire among teenage and pre-teenage girls, they also added millions of sales onto releases made subsequently with his brothers. When Donny, Wayne, Merrill, Alan and Jay descended on Britain in 1972, the world was gripped by Osmondmania.

But it didn't stop there. If Donny appealed to little sister and the others to big sister and mum, what about big brother and dad? Fortunately, Mr and Mrs Osmond were a veritable child factory, and the next to come off the production line was, conveniently enough, a highly attractive daughter called Marie. 'Paper Roses' established her, but it was with brother Donny that she had most success. The siblings were given a syrupy TV series of their own, which served as a vehicle to give them Top 10 hits such as 'I'm Leaving It Up To You' and 'Morning Side Of The Mountain'.

By the mid-1970s, the popularity of the Osmonds was inevitably beginning to wane, but the final nail in the coffin was the introduction into the firmament of Little Jimmy. This alarming-looking child scored a Number 1 hit with an excruciating song called 'Long Haired Lover From Liverpool', but for most observers he was just one Osmond too far.

Gob On You: Malcolm McLaren And The Punk Revolution

By the mid-1970s, pop music had evolved into a corpulent, ungainly beast which wallowed in its own excesses and churned out little in return. Bands like Led Zeppelin toured the world in their own Boeing 747; Pink Floyd released tedious, drug-fuelled 'concept' albums; Emerson, Lake and Palmer and Elton John sold out 100,000 seat arenas so big that no one could see them on stage; ELO performed with the London Philharmonic; and even The Who, who once hoped to die before they got old, turned 30 and produced a staggeringly pompous rock opera. 'Bohemian Rhapsody', a seven-minute single by Queen, was the biggest-selling record of the period and eloquently sums up how rough-and-ready rock had debauched itself with theatrical, overblown swagger.

In Britain, the state of the music industry was summed up every week on New Faces, where Mickie Most and Tony Hatch smugly dismissed up-and-coming acts, whilst growing unfeasibly rich churning out bubblegum pop with little or no intrinsic worth. In the USA, the bankruptcy of musical ideas in a country which had invented rock 'n'

The Monkees. It was also manufactured pop's finest hour to date and, in Malcolm McLaren, it had unearthed its brashest exponent.

In the early 1970s, McLaren first displayed his knack for creating publicity when, as manager of the ailing New York Dolls, he persuaded the band to forsake their glam-rock image and embrace Communist-chic instead. Their subsequent concerts, in which they performed in fetching red rubber trousers in front of a hammer and sickle flag, got them the headlines McLaren craved, while doing little to prolong their fading career. By the time the Dolls were imploding, McLaren was already back in London, where the next step of his career would take off.

At an early stage McLaren, although no musician, had identified and absorbed the business lessons of the industry. In the self-congratulatory movie *The Great Rock 'N' Roll Swindle*, he would make great show of these supposed tenets while giving the impression that he had actually invented them himself. In fact, there was only one basic rule that McLaren mastered and it was the oldest in the book. It was also the most important: the fact that record sales were dependent on column centimetres rather than musical ability. However, he would later admit, 'Plagiarism is what the world is all about. If you didn't start seeing things and stealing them because you were so inspired by them, you'd be stupid.'

His experiences with The New York Dolls had convinced him that his philosophy was right, but that America was not the right place to put his ideas into action. Britain in the mid-1970s, however, had it all: a smug establishment, an increasingly disillusioned underclass and, crucially, a voracious, conservative media. McLaren's genius was playing off all three against each other to the maximum effect.

'Throughout the glam period, McLaren had been watching the growing number of disenfranchised teenagers who called themselves skinheads,' recalls Simon Napier-Bell. 'They shaved their heads and bashed up Pakistanis. Their lives were empty and negative, which was what made them so attractive. By presenting his new group as anti-social monsters, he would grab the respect of these disenfranchised kids and turn them into a captive audience.'

'You Ever Get The Feeling You Been Ripped Off?'

McLaren's new group was, of course, The Sex Pistols. 'The idea of the name of the Sex Pistols was a sort of sexy young assassins,' he explained. '*Pistol* meaning "a gun" and *pistol* meaning "a penis". [Johnny] Rotten said, "Why can't we just have the name Sex?" And I thought, well, the name Sex…you're just not saying it all boy, you know, get it out! Sex, that could mean anything. Sex Pistols, and you're active immediately.'

The name itself was calculated to generate headlines in the ultra-conservative Daily Mail, but this was only the beginning of a market-

The Sex Pistols: punk iconoclasts or just a cynical marketing ploy by their manager Malcolm McLaren?

ing scam breathtaking in its audacity and in its simplicity. Almost everything about the Pistols was a sham: the band was portrayed as a group of mindless louts, when in fact its lead singer John Lydon – promptly renamed Johnny Rotten – was an intelligent middle-class boy from Finsbury Park, and its bass player Glen Matlock was a highly proficient musician and songwriter whose Pistols back catalogue, which includes 'God Save The Queen' and 'Pretty Vacant', are rightly regarded as classics. Guitarist Steve Jones and drummer Paul Cook had both dabbled in petty crime, but McLaren talked them up in the press as if they were both hardened cons. Matlock would later be replaced by Sid Vicious, whose only talents lay in heroin consumption and self-mutilation, but this was an entirely cosmetic decision by McLaren in order to crank up the outrage factor when it had begun to flag.

An indication of how revolutionary McLaren's creation was is pro-vided by the fact that in November 1975, when the Pistols made their

nice fat severance cheque for £50,000. He was also in the process of closing a new contract deal with A&M worth a cool £75,000.

But not everyone was fooled. Captain Sensible, bass player with contemporaries The Damned, recalled his reaction to the long-awaited release of 'Anarchy In The UK'.

'When we heard it we all pissed ourselves with laughter. It sounded like some redundant Bad Company out take with old man Steptoe singing over the top.'

While McLaren was doing his best to make The Sex Pistols the most infamous band in history, a huge merchandising campaign had already been set in motion aimed at milking the punk phenomenon for all it was worth. McLaren's sometime lover, the designer Vivienne Westwood, came up with a fashion line consisting of ripped clothes held together with safety pins. To publicise the release of the Pistols' 'God Save The Queen', a poster was designed which showed HRH with a safety pin through her nose. Crude slogans such as 'No Future' and 'Anarchy' were steam-pressed onto sleeveless black T-shirts in lettering that resembled a kidnapper's ransom note. Lapel badges were produced by the boxload and worn on school blazers as a symbol of rebellion. As Westwood pointed out, 'There is nothing young people like more than having people against them and knowing they look good.'

'Anarchy In The UK' may have been punk's clarion call, but there was nothing anarchic about the way in which it was flogged to the public. It was big business, pure and simple, from top to bottom. Romantics claim that punk enabled kids to pick up a guitar, learn two chords and make a record, but even the independent record labels had bills to pay. Punk was the new vogue, and it was in their interests to speculate on new talent in the hope of unearthing the next Damned, Clash or Stranglers. They were just as ruthless when it came to ditching bands who didn't have money-spinning potential – and they numbered in the hundreds.

Charlie Harper, ageing lead singer of one-hit wonders the UK Subs admitted the truth of the matter when he said, 'To me punk was an excuse for fanatics to have their say, people like me who never had a chance before, people who have just been laughed at. Blokes like me who've just been through life being sneered at. When punk came along it was the best thing that ever happened to me. I was accepted.'

In the end, punk was like any other manufactured fad – a triumph of style over substance, hype and hysteria squeezed till the pips squeaked. It was encapsulated by the fate of The Sex Pistols who, after being dumped by A&M a week after signing a contract (and earning McLaren another £40,000 pay off), flipped one last splendid V-sign at the establishment by releasing 'God Save the Queen' in the middle of Jubilee year; and disintegrated amid acrimony a few weeks later, with Rotten asking an audience in San Francisco, 'You ever get the feeling you been ripped off?' before walking out on the band.

In the end even McLaren seemed devoid of ideas. Bringing the remaining Pistols together with train robber Ronnie Biggs for a single called 'Cosh The Driver' smacked of desperation and the band were pretty much yesterday's news when, in 1978, Sid Vicious was charged with murdering his girlfriend and, while awaiting trial, overdosed on heroin.

Yet this is not to say punk did not leave a legacy. Musically, its asskicking, guitar-based thrash would provide the creative impetus for New Wave, and its raw echo continues to surface even today – Nirvana sound like The Exploited might have done, had they been able to play their instruments and had a brain cell between them. But punk's main importance in the scheme of things was that it shook the music industry out of its MOR torpor and provided a timely slap in the face for the major record companies, whose stranglehold was prised loose by young independent labels like Stiff and 2Tone. It ushered in a whole batch of much-needed new blood onto the music scene, bands who wouldn't have had a look-in previously. It was like a huge version of *New Faces* that served the purpose of unearthing a handful of genuine diamonds from thousands of hopefuls.

Disco Inferno

America watched the punk outbreak in Britain with an appalled fascination, and was relieved when it died out without causing too much of a fuss. This is not to say the US was bypassed entirely. The Cramps were the leading lights of a mainly New York-based cell of punk-rockers, but were too Gothic and theatrical to stand up to comparison with British punk bands. The Dead Kennedys, from San Francisco, were outrage merchants along the same lines as the Pistols, but with more wit: songs like 'California Über Alles' and 'Holiday In Cambodia' combined top-notch punk thrash with wicked satire. Overall, however, the US music scene remained the exclusive territory of turgid MOR bands like Chicago, REO Speedwagon and Air Supply, whose stadium-rock-based ballads did wonders for the sales of cigarette lighters and mullet haircuts. The death of Elvis Presley in 1977 – rock 'n' roll's greatest name found bloated and drug addled on his toilet floor – eloquently summed up the state of the industry.

Europe had provided one-hit wonders Pussycat ('Mississippi') from Holland and the considerably more enduring Swedes, Abba, in 1974, but its contribution to punk and the New Wave scene had consisted mainly of Plastic Bertrand, who wore tight jeans and red shoes and proved that at least some Belgians have a sense of humour. Thankfully a continent seemingly bereft of anything more daring than 'oompah' music was about to redeem itself by inventing what was, in its way, as much a musical revolution as punk. For, while Britain was pogoing, the rest of the world was about to go four-to-the-floor disco dancing.

One of the leading architects of disco was an Italian record producer called Giorgio Moroder. It was not much fun being a continental

The Village People

With American gay clubs providing much of the impetus to the disco boom of the late 1970s, it was only a matter of time before the phenomenon was given human form. The most extraordinary thing about The Village People is that so few people outside the gay community twigged that they were actually gay. It was a cause of huge amusement when the US Navy requested if it could use their second hit 'In The Navy' as a backing track for its recruitment campaign.

The group was the concept of French record producer Jacques Morali, one of the main players in the burgeoning Eurodisco movement. In 1977, having already secured a contract and commissioned songwriters to come up with a raft of suitably innuendo-packed songs including 'San Francisco (You've Got Me)' and 'Macho Man', Morali set about recruiting a motley bunch of dancers, actors and session singers to make up the group. Next he dressed them up as crude gay stereotypes: construction worker, cop, biker, Red Indian, cowboy and GI.

'I thought that it is fantastic to see the cowboy, the Indian, the construction worker with other men around,' Morali said in an interview at the height of the group's late-1970s popularity. 'And also, I thought to myself that gay people have no group, nobody to personalise the gay people.'

Their early singles hovered around the periphery of the charts, but the group exploded in 1978 with the release of 'YMCA'. Despite containing such thinly-disguised gay aspirations as young men hanging out with all the boys and having showers together, the straight population lapped it up, enchanted by its thumping rhythm, irresistible hook, and the arm-waving dance which became a regular sight on dancefloors around the world.

The next single was 'In The Navy', which told of the great time young men could have together while sailing the seven seas. Again it was a world-wide hit – although ironically the backlash that was starting to rumble about the Village People was emanating from the gay community, which was tiring of the joke and starting to resent the stereotype. The encounter with the US Navy had also backfired: the secret was out, and Middle America railed at the fact that it had been suckered by 'a bunch of faggots'.

Morali saw what was happening, and the next two singles were the sexually ambivalent disco releases 'Can't Stop The Music' and 'Go West'. The group were also featured in a dreadful movie that did them no good whatsoever. It was too late. The writing was on the wall, and the chart hits dried up – although 'YMCA' remains a disco standard.

'Village People were quintessential American stereotypes, cartoons come to life, live action figures,' says music critic Will Grega. 'The group took the risk unprecedented in music history of short-circuiting their careers by being unabashedly gay, masculine and sexual. Even though the songs were not blatantly gay, they were certainly open to interpretation.'

*The Village People were designer camp –
but even the US Navy didn't twig until it
was too late*

'Europe has somehow taken a lead in making the music,' Moroder said. 'Perhaps we just had the correct professional attitudes.'

The arrival of this irresistibly catchy music led to a boom in dancing which hadn't been seen since the early 1960s. Suddenly, the discotheque was the place to be on a Saturday night and punters couldn't get enough of the new sound. It was also enthusiastically embraced by DJs, who found that because Moroder's so-called 'four to the floor' backbeat was pretty much standard issue on new records, they were able to seamlessly mix and remix different tracks on the turntable, enabling the music to go on indefinitely without a break.

But the people who loved disco most were the record producers, who discovered that they could quickly and easily create unlimited hits using only a drum machine, a synth and whichever session musicians happened to be handy to add the vocal track. It was manufactured pop at its purest – music created by a machine, and artists who never toured or made personal appearances, or indeed had anything to do with the record once it had been released.

attractive session singers. The resulting group was called Chic, and the name totally summed up their innovative brand of cool and sophisticated music. Here, for the first time, was disco you could play at dinner parties, and the band pressed home the point by appearing on their record sleeves in expensive suits and lounging in white-painted loft apartments. The Chic sound was instantly recognisable: Rodgers' chopping guitar and Edwards' rangy basslines were under-scored by the relentless beat provided by drummer Tony Thompson. In 1978, the wonderful 'Le Freak' became the biggest-selling single in Atlantic's history, and was supplemented by 'I Want Your Love' and 'Good Times'.

Rodgers and Edwards were suddenly in demand. They penned 'Upside Down', which provided Diana Ross with an unexpected chart hit, and (with 'Spacer') gave session singer Sheila B Devotion a chart-topper which wouldn't have looked out of place on a Chic album.

C'est Chic: Nile Rodgers and Bernard Edwards created their own brand of ultra-smooth New York disco music

Their favourite project, however, was undoubtedly Sister Sledge. Joan, Kim and Kathy Sledge had been little more than jobbing back-ing singers for most of the 1970s until they came under the influence of Rodgers and Edwards. Hardly the most glamorous trio – teenager Kathy's teeth braces provided a constant talking point – the boys nevertheless provided them with a string of transatlantic smashes including 'We Are Family', 'He's The Greatest Dancer' and 'Lost In Music'. The music was pure Chic, but the Sledges' downhome family charm (and, yes, Kathy's braces) gave it the human touch that was sometimes lacking.

After a ropey start, the 1970s were coming to an end on an optimistic note. The punk and disco explosions had given rise to a plethora of new talent and the last years of the decade saw the rise of acts like The Police, Blondie, The Boomtown Rats, Dire Straits, The Jam, Elvis Costello, as well as the welcome demise of dinosaurs like ELP, Supertramp and Led Zeppelin.

The industry still found it hard to shake its bad habits, however. Despite a glut of excellent bands who were able to write and perform their own material, certain record companies were still determined to create their own. The Knack, for example, were a grotesque facsimile of a New Wave band from California, who fell under the control of Mike Chapman and inflicted 'My Sharona' on an undeserving world. The Goombay Dance Band proved that, even if it had helped to create disco, Europe still had an uncanny ability to create unbearable Eurotrash. In her mid-30s, US session singer Toni Basil somehow man-aged to keep a straight face as she danced around like a teenage pompom girl while singing about 'Mickey'.

In the UK, Malcolm McLaren blotted his copybook somewhat by creating Bow Wow Wow, whose sole selling point was their lead singer, a 14-year-old half-Burmese girl McLaren had spotted working in his local laundrette. Even gimmicks like producing singles on cassette tape with suggestive titles like 'Sexy Eiffel Towers' could not save the band from almost immediate oblivion, and the whole exercise proved how badly McLaren had lost his touch.

The nucleus of Bow Wow Wow was three former members of Adam And The Ants. The lead singer of the Ants was a desperate post-punk wannabe named Stuart Goddard who, in 1978, had actually paid McLaren £1,000 for advice on how to become a star. McLaren told him to become an Apache, pinched his band and trousered the money. Incredibly, Goddard took his advice and his subsequent success set a precedent that would hang over the early years of the 1980s like a perfumed cloud.

Taking the Mickey: Toni Basil was in her mid-30s when she appeared as a teenage cheerleader

Bow Wow Wow

Just when Malcolm McLaren appeared to be yesterday's entrepreneur, following the shambolic demise of The Sex Pistols, the genial redhead bounced back in 1980 with a typically unrepentant, and for some stomach-churning, piece of headline-grabbing.

Washing his underpants one day at his local laundrette in Kilburn, north London, McLaren became infatuated with one of the staff and resolved to turn her into a star. The fact that Burmese-born Myant Aye was only 14 would prove no object – indeed it added to the exotic Far East spice around which he planned to base his new creation. The girl became Annabella Lwin, her fresh-faced looks were topped off with a striking mohican hairdo, and she was dispatched to the recording studio with three former members of Adam And The Ants.

The group began in relatively low-key style – at least compared to what McLaren had up his sleeve for them. The single 'C30, C60, C90 Go!' was an Ants-style thrash which glorified the teen craze of home taping, and was followed up by a cassette-only 'Your Cassette Pet', which contained the first hint of what was to follow. One track featured Annabella crooning suggestively about wrapping her legs around 'Sexy Eiffel Towers' and had the desired effect of getting the group on the pages of newspapers alongside words like 'teenage sex' and 'paedophilia'.

The foundations laid, the following year Bow Wow Wow released their first album entitled *See Jungle! See Jungle! Go Join Your Gang, Yeah! City All Over! Go Ape Crazy!* The album cover featured a nude Annabella in a recreation of Manet's 1863 *Déjeuner Sur L'Herbe* ('Lunch On The Grass') and caused more of a splash than the record itself. This, of course, was precisely what McLaren wanted – and on the strength of the controversy, the single 'Go Wild In The Country' became a big UK hit. This was quickly followed by the equally suggestive Top 10 hit 'I Want Candy', but interest in the group was already beginning to wane, especially Annabella's, who found the paedo publicity generated in her name somewhat disturbing.

In 1983, McLaren appointed a second lead singer to the band, a recruit from the burgeoning London club scene who went by the name of Lieutenant Lush. But within weeks Bow Wow Wow was consigned to the bubblegum bin. Annabella would make an unsuccessful return as a solo artist in 1985, but by then she and the rest of the pop world had been eclipsed by her old partner Lieutenant Lush who, now known as Boy George, was making global headlines with Culture Club.

While Bow Wow Wow had proved that Malcolm McLaren could still do it, the overtly cynical nature of the creation showed that he could no longer do it as well as he once could. There was none of the mischief that typified the Pistols, none of the élan. Instead of a fond memory, the group merely left a sour taste in the mouth and an uncomfortable feeling of being soiled. McLaren was right to pick up on the fact that sex sells – and especially teenage sex – but when planeloads of perverts regularly travelled to the Far East in search of underage girls, the exploitation of 14-year-old Annabella Lwin seemed beyond the pale. It would not be the last the pop world would see of McLaren, but for a while he was wise to keep his head down.

Teen porn accusations abounded about Bow Wow Wow's 14-year-old singer Annabel Lwin. In the end, even she found it too much to take

The 1980s would herald the glory years of bubblegum pop, when all the lessons of the previous 30 years came together in the kind of natural harmony that the popsters themselves could only dream about. There was Thatcherism in the UK and Reaganomics in the US; it was an era which provided a rich furrow of material for po-faced, socially switched-on musos to plough, but an even richer one for the industry's newest generation of pop capitalists and entrepreneurs.

Crucially, it was also the era of MTV. Here was a concept Larry Parnes and co would have loved: music TV that, unlike what had gone before, was accessible 24 hours a day and therefore desperate to show your act over and over to fill the long empty hours. Videos, as Simon Napier-Bell points out, were 'basically just advertisements [which] became an accepted form of entertainment at dance clubs, pubs, shops and shopping malls'.

Video became a breeding ground for moviemakers, just as disco had made stars out of the disc jockeys, and as a consequence, the music became even less important than the image. And while video did not, in the words of the Buggles, actually kill the radio star, in the 1980s it ushered him down a back alley, kicked seven bells out of him and stole his wallet and credit-cards. It did this by horribly exposing one of the unfortunate truisms of the pop music industry - that good looks do not always go hand-in-hand with musical talent.

One of the major songwriting talents at the turn of the decade was Christopher Cross, who scored massive hits in the US with 'Ride Like The Wind' and 'Sailing'. But his career effectively stalled the moment he appeared on MTV and revealed that he looked like an overweight McDonald's burger-flipper. Meanwhile Bananarama, who sang like a train going through a tunnel, looked good on video and would become the biggest-selling all-girl group in the world, eclipsing even The Supremes.

Lipstick, Powder And Paint: New Romantics And Gender Benders

In the early months of the 1980s, no one benefited more from the video boom than Adam And The Ants. The nucleus of the band had actually been around since the punk era, when they had been singularly unsuccessful. But they – and in particular their singer, Stuart Goddard – were nothing if not determined. As an avid fan of The Sex Pistols, Goddard had absorbed the lesson that a good image was far more important in getting noticed than a good song. He also knew that there was no one in the world at the time who had more of an instinct for image creation than Malcolm McLaren.

McLaren's advice to Goddard to model himself on an Apache warrior may or may not have been flippant. Certainly,

me want to puke'. But Weller, who had spent his years with The Jam modelling himself on the preening Mods of the 1960s, and would subsequently reinvent himself in the 1980s as an ultra-cool updated version of a character from Brideshead Revisited, knew all too well that showbusiness was anything but crap. In the 1980s, it was the fashion.

In London in the early 1980s, trendy West End nightclubs were jammed to the rafters with fey young things who had gleefully raided their mum's make-up bags and ransacked secondhand clothes shops for a look that became known as New Romantic. In many ways it was a throwback to the punk era, but the difference was that, while punks went in for self-mutilation and outfits that made them look like refugees, the New Romantics – as the name suggests – modelled themselves on 18th-century dandies. 'We got a tag "The New Romantics" and in a way we were,' said Spandau Ballet's Gary Kemp. 'We were against the kind of dourness of punk.'

The groups that emerged from this period had similarly grandiose names like Classix Nouveaux and Spandau Ballet, Visage, Heaven 17 and Cabaret Voltaire – deliberately dispensing with the traditional band prefix 'The' as if the idea of being associated with rock 'n' roll was simply too tawdry for words. The majority of these groups were stylists first and musicians a distant second, poseurs who seemed quite happy to become one-hit wonders as long as it guaranteed them the chance of showing off their look on *Top Of The Pops*, *The Tube* or *MTV*. A Flock Of Seagulls became an international talking point not because of their record 'I Ran', but because of their lead singer's extraordinary haircut, which resembled a wedge of brie attached to his skull.

What interested the TV and record producers of the day was not the music, which was bland and ordinary, but the look. New Romantic groups got a level of exposure in the first years of the decade which their talent did not deserve, because they were regarded as such an extraordinary slice of youth culture. Marilyn, for example, was a stunning blond with cheekbones to die for until she opened her mouth and revealed that she was, in fact, a hefty 6ft (183cm) transvestite who had been invited into the studio by his pal Boy George, cut a record called 'Calling Your Name', made a few bob and, more importantly, made a video.

It was as if the glam rockers had returned with a vengeance – although the tabloid press preferred the more pungent description 'gender benders'.

The biggest name at the time, having assumed the mantle from Adam Ant, was Boy George. He was also the biggest gender bender. Born plain George O'Dowd, his yen for stardom had been encouraged by the hedonistic club scene in London, where he was at last able to drop his boring suburban existence, stick on a ball gown and some lipstick and become one of its leading lights. When Malcolm McLaren was looking to boost the flagging fortunes of Bow Wow Wow, he chose George – then known as Lieutenant Lush – as a foil for

A Flock Of Seagulls: 'lead singer's extraordinary haircut resembled a wedge of brie attached to his skull'

Annabella Lwin. When his natural flamboyance began to steal the show he was ditched, but it was only a matter of time before he carved out his new position as the foremost act of the New Romantic era. Although George possessed no musical background, he was blessed with an extraordinary soul voice which would later earn him comparisons with the great Smokey Robinson. Together with the experienced musicians in Culture Club and producer Steve Levine, he was able to express himself as a first-rate songwriter. And, of course, his appearance and natural ability to court publicity (he memorably said he'd rather have a cup of tea than sex), made him an instant star. When he first appeared on TV singing 'Do You Really Want To Hurt Me' in 1982, viewers were either appalled or infatuated. Nearly all of them found themselves tapping their feet, however.

Sigue Hell

But you didn't just have to be a gender bender to be able to score a hit in the early 1980s. Like glam rock, to which it was compared, the image-led New Romantic scene enabled musicians who had been around the block a few times to have one last tilt at chart success. As a teenager in Colchester, Essex, in the late 1970s, writer Giles Smith used to watch with awe the guitarist with local pub band Fusion. His

name was Nick Kershaw. In his book Lost In Music, Smith recalls catching sight of Kershaw in the mid-1980s on the eve of the singer's metamorphosis into the teen idol Nik Kershaw.

Rampant commercialism: Sigue Sigue Sputnik set out to make a mint, and found more than enough suckers

> *First there was the hair – all spiky and bright blond as if a small bomb containing bleach had gone off on his head, the de rigueur 1980s pop-star plumage. And then there were the clothes. No more wearisome waistcoats, no more duff ties. He was wearing a tiny black jacket with some complicated fastenings, and a pair of black drainpipe jeans which bottomed out into a pair of pointy boots... The haircut and the grimly fashionable threads were courtesy of MCA, who were right at that moment priming Kershaw, ready to detonate him and his new hair in the teen market.*

The period also saw a thankfully brief renaissance by the dregs of the punk movement. Johnny Rotten reappeared as John Lydon with his new band Public Image Ltd and enjoyed a modicum of success based largely on fond memories of his previous incarnation. Meanwhile, Tony James – significantly a former member of faux-punk band Generation X with Billy Idol – pushed the bounds of credibility to the limit with his latest creation, the ghastly Sigue Sigue Sputnik. Having failed to

Kajagoogoo: crazy name, crazy hair, crazy guys – but consigned to oblivion after the mandatory 18 months of hysteria

Kajagoogoo

Although almost no one would admit to liking them at the time, Kajagoogoo would become one of the top-selling bubblegum acts of the early 1980s, and are still one of the most fondly remembered today. They were a prime example of a bunch of no-hopers transformed by image makers, video exposure and clever production into a viable, if short-lived, chart proposition.

Long before their first and best-known single, 'Too Shy', reached the charts, the marketing men at EMI had already begun the task of creating a myth around the band, who had begun life as four wannabes from Leighton Buzzard, Hertfordshire. Their name alone was enough to assure them newspaper coverage. In interviews, the group followed the record company baloney about Kajagoogoo representing the innocent utterances of the new born child, but everyone knew it was codswallop. The lead singer was called Limahl, which sounded exotic and interesting until it was revealed to be an anagram of his real name, Christopher Hamill.

In the studio, they went to work with Duran Duran's talented keyboard maestro Nick Rhodes, and the end result was an album of typically smooth electropop combined with the fretless basslines that had become in vogue ever since Japan's Mick Karn had popularised them a few months earlier.

The band's look – in particular, Limahl's albino porcupine hairstyle, and bassist Nick Beggs's candyfloss construction – was an immediate talking point, and their cleverly filmed videos did the trick of distracting attention from Limahl's vocal limitations.

Three Top 10 singles later, the band were history, citing the usual musical differences but, in reality, grateful to the bubblegum machine for helping them last two hits longer than they probably deserved. After the break-up, Limahl's solo career predictably flopped and Beggs bizarrely washed up with a Christian folk band before re-joining the fold as an executive with A&M Records.

'U Can't Touch This': he had the world at his feet, but MC Hammer went from riches to rags overnight

MC Hammer

After failing as a professional baseball player, taking a college course in communications and spending several years in the US Navy, 24-year-old Stanley Burrell decided there had to be a faster way to make a buck. He found it by pilfering rap music from the ghettos, buying himself a pair of unfeasibly baggy trousers, and signing a staggering $750,000 record deal with Capitol, who marketed the newly renamed MC Hammer as rap's first superstar.

The 1989 single 'U Can't Touch This', whose catchy riff was half-inched from the Rick James song 'Super Freak', featured one of the first successful examples of sampling which, allied with some admittedly spectacular choreography (and *those* trousers) sent it rocketing up the charts on the back of wall-to-wall MTV coverage. His album *Please Hammer Don't Hurt 'Em* stayed at the top of the US charts for a whopping 21 weeks.

Hammer's already bulging coffers were further enhanced when he signed sponsorship deals with British Knights footwear and Pepsi, and as the 1980s marched into the 1990s Hammer had established himself as the first all-rapping, all-dancing franchise. Any complaints that his music was secondhand and his rapping was little more than sloganeering were swept away on a tidal wave of merchandising and TV exposure. Such was his appeal that he became the first pop star since The Osmonds to be given his own cartoon series, *Hammerman*. In Los Angeles and Fremont, he was regarded as such an outstanding role model for black youth that MC Hammer Days were celebrated.

The backlash, when it inevitably came, was swift and devastating, and came not from the press – who would have loved to have found him snorting coke or frequenting with gangstas – but from the public, who abruptly stopped buying his records and going to his concerts. It seemed that the exposure that had made him a global superstar had become *over*exposure, and people were now sick to death of him. When reports began to circulate that Hammer faced financial ruin after the failure of his 1992 world tour, the press at last had something to go for, and they went for him with a vengeance. Despite a number of image changes, including one ill-conceived stab at becoming a gangsta-rapper, Hammer's career at the top was all but over, and these days he spends much of his time as a born-again preacher.

But, while Hammer's out-and-out artistic commercialism was too much for some to stomach, his anti-drug and anti-violence message was never anything but genuine, and today seems refreshing compared to the 'kill a cop' exhortations of the legions of Uzi-toting gangsta-rappers who followed him.

But now it was a matter of pride.

The starmaker in the 1980s was the appropriately named Maurice Starr, a Boston-based Svengali who was responsible for creating two of the major boy bands of the period, New Edition and New Kids On The Block.

New Edition were as aptly monikered as their manager, being in essence the latest incarnation of such black teen singing groups as Frankie Lymon and The Teenagers and, in particular, the Jackson 5. Based around the piping, pre-pubescent voice of 13 year-old Bobby Brown, they hit the big time with a piece of fluff called 'Candy Girl' in 1983. But the band – and Brown in particular – were keen to expand their repertoire and style from the lucrative but limiting bubblegum that Starr wanted them to perform. They were very interested in the nascent 'ghetto' sounds of hiphop and rap, and, after firing Starr, they went on to experiment briefly with the style before Brown left for his own highly successful solo career.

Starr, meanwhile, had scoured Boston for replacements for New Edition and come up with five suitable white boys: brothers Jordan and Jonathan Knight, Danny Wood, Joey MacIntyre and Donnie Wahlberg. Ironically, the group took its name from a rap song called 'New Kids On The Block'. The song had been unearthed by Starr, who had belatedly taken on board the latest trend in youth music after being axed by New Edition, and in 1986 the group did well among white teen audiences with their blend of rap and pop, described unkindly (if not inaccurately) by one commentator as 'pretendy nigger music'.

But rap was not the only trend that Starr recognised as being increasingly prevalent among teen audiences. He watched Madonna wannabes and was astonished to see girls as young as 6 or 7 walking about in torn fishnet stockings and slut eyeliner. It was pure sex, and if that's what they wanted then that's what he would give them. Ten years before, The Osmonds and the Jackson 5 had come on stage wearing smart matching suits; now New Kids On The Block sent their pre-teen fans into ecstasy by exposing finely honed six-packs, grabbing their bulging crotches and thrusting their pelvises suggestively. As with all things in pop, it was nothing new – David Bowie used to mime oral sex with Mick Ronson's guitar on stage, and the ageing Mick Jagger still pranced around stage in tights – but for bubblegum popsters and their army of fans it was a revelation.

The Hit Men

After the simpering androgyny of the New Romantic years, youngsters in the UK fell on sexy American exports like a pack of ravenous animals. The obvious next step for the movers and shakers of the British music industry should have been to clear the decks of the lipgloss brigade and begin scouring the nation for raunch. They did the former: New Romantics were ditched almost overnight. Yet, instead of creating a raft of home-grown Madonnas and New Kids On The

New Edition: raised to be the next Jackson 5, but they had other ideas

Compared to such honed girl groups as The Supremes or even the Three Degrees, Bananarama looked like three tone-deaf girls singing at a hen party. Some say their amateurism was all part of their charm, something the girls themselves readily agreed with.

'I think our charm was that we weren't too professional,' recalled Keren. 'I mean, we couldn't be because we didn't know what we were doing. So I think the fact that we tried to do dance routines that always went wrong on Top Of The Pops, I think that was really amusing. And we always laughed about it on stage, we didn't think, "Oh my God, we've gone wrong, that's really bad," we just didn't mind failing in public.'

Others would argue, less charitably, that it was a scandal that they were allowed to get so far without being rumbled.

The girls first came to prominence as backing singers for Fun Boy Three, a band started by Terry Hall after he left The Specials in 1982. Hall then provided backing for Bananarama's début single 'Really Saying Something', which zoomed into the UK Top 5. Their early appeal is understandable: Boy George and Marilyn wore more make-up than Bananarama, and the group's embarrassed, shuffling performances on TV and their unpretentious appearance struck a chord with pop fans at the nihilistic height of the New Romantic movement. What is less easy to understand is how the success continued. But continue it did, throughout the mid-1980s, with a string of hits including 'Shy Boy', 'Robert De Niro's Waiting' and 'Na Na Hey Hey Kiss Him Goodbye'. It was only when Bananarama got political, with a song about the Troubles in Northern Ireland, that eyebrows were raised. The song, 'Rough Justice', bombed in the charts as fans found it difficult to reconcile such a serious message being sung by a group called Bananarama.

There it might have ended, had Pete Waterman not taken them under his wing in 1986. He quickly dismissed any political agenda the band might have been toying with, and instead relaunched their career with an injection of pure SAW pop, starting with a spirited remake of Shocking Blue's 'Venus,' which got to the top of the US charts, and culminating with 'Love In The First Degree', which confirmed Bananarama as the most successful girl group of all time. In 1988, Siobhan left to form the drearily pretentious Shakespears Sister and the game was up.

By then, however, Stock, Aitken and Waterman had long proved what they were capable of when it came to plugging into the pop psyche, not only of the UK but across the rest of the world. Their bouncy, synthesised sound was as instantly recognisable as that of Phil Spector and Motown, and it provided the signature tune for a host of manufactured acts throughout the 1980s.

Two of their biggest home-grown success stories were the Appleby sisters, Mel and Kim, and Rick Astley. Both in their own way showed the infallible power of the SAW bubblegum machine in its glory years.

Top-selling threesome Bananarama: was there no beginning to their talents?

Mel and Kim were all about fun, love and money, but tragedy struck when Mel contracted cancer

Mel and Kim were a couple of models from the East End of London whose irrepressible Cockney charm and not inconsiderable talent as dancers and singers made them a ready-made double act to be fed into the production line. Waterman didn't have to rack his brains too hard in order to sell them as party girls interested in having a good time, and the point was reinforced with hits like 'Showing Out (Get Fresh At The Weekend)', 'FLM (Fun, Love, Money)' and 'Respectable'. Who knows what they might have achieved, had Mel not been struck down by cancer at a shockingly young age.

Astley, on the other hand, was a painfully shy redhead from the sleepy Lancashire suburb of Newton-le-Willows, who possessed a remarkably strong voice. This by itself would probably have garnered him a degree of pop stardom, but Waterman made great play of the fact that Astley had been working as a tape engineer and general factotum at SAW's London studios before being given a chance at cutting his own disc. His success with songs like 'Never Gonna Give You Up' and 'Together Forever', which both went to Number 1 in both the UK and the US, was touted as evidence of Waterman's Midas touch – which in many respects it was.

Around the same time, Waterman was appearing in a late-night TV show entitled *The Hit Man And Her*, in which he and Michaela Strachan toured nightclubs allegedly in search of new talent. Although to the casual observer it looked like the youthful Strachan was being accompanied by her dad, it got the point across that Waterman was the self-appointed kingpin of pop, the star-maker, the Larry Parnes of the 1980s.

It is a comparison that Waterman has always strenuously denied. He said, 'The major difference between myself and Parnes is that Parnes treated everybody with total disrespect. He treated everyone as though they were stupid. He really believed you could con people all the time. He had no respect for his artists: ordering Marty Wilde to shove toilet rolls down his trousers! I'm the total opposite.

'I'd love to say to some of my artists,"Shut your fucking mouth or I'll knock your head off." But I'm not like that. Even when they're talking

Shy boy: Rick Astley used to make the tea for the stars until Pete Waterman made him a chart-topper

Little Kylie Minogue had been a fixture of Australian soap operas since she was knee-high to a kookaburra. But, while shows like *The Sullivans* and *Skyways* made her a household name in Oz, she was a complete unknown anywhere else. In 1986, aged 18, she joined the cast of *Neighbours* as feisty mechanic Charlene and, a year later, she decided to follow the trend of a number of her fellow actors by trying her hand at the music business. A warbly rendition of 'The Loco-Motion' performed at a big Aussie Rules football game should have been the beginning and end of it, but Kylie was in luck.

In 1987, British TV had begun all-day schedules and was consequently desperate to fill the dead daytime hours. *Neighbours* was just one of a number of cheap imports which fitted the bill, and its daily lunchtime screenings became cult viewing among students and schoolkids alike. In a cast dominated by older actors, Kylie's impact – along with that of Jason Donovan – was enormous. The canny Waterman, who always had an ear to the ground when it came to the latest youth trends, invited her across to the UK to sing the SAW-produced 'I Should Be So Lucky', and to everyone's astonishment – not least Kylie's – the single rocketed to Number 1.

It was only a matter of time before Kylie's *Neighbours* co-star Jason Donovan was invited to the party. Blond and good-looking, he not only provided the perfect male counterpoint to Kylie, but his soap character Scott was also in the midst of a 'Will they, won't they?' romance with Charlene. With Waterman skilfully manipulating the UK media, fans became unable to distinguish the difference between TV fiction

Kylie Minogue: 'an antiseptic swab' – but also one of bubblegum pop's greatest exponents

Jason Donovan was tipped for enduring stardom, but gay allegations and drug use wrecked his career as a teen idol

Kylie Minogue and
Jason Donovan

and reality. The romance between Kylie and Jason therefore became accepted fact and did wonders for their record sales. The fact that Jason's voice, especially in the early years, was like a foghorn did little to prevent singles like 'Too Many Broken Hearts' zooming into the charts.

Modern Kylie fans, who know her as a disco diva with a permanently pouting backside, would barely recognise her mid-1980s incarnation. Back then, she was a toothy, clean-cut girl who wore nice dresses and was the epitome of what every mother would want her son to bring home – 'an antiseptic swab' as one critic unkindly described her. And her popularity was universal. Her second release, 'Got To Be Certain', reached Number 2 in the UK but hit the top spot in Australia, Belgium, New Zealand, Israel, Hong Kong and Finland, and reached the Top 10 throughout Europe and Asia. Hastily re-released versions of 'Loco-Motion' and 'I Should Be So Lucky' hit the American market like a storm, while her album Kylie continued the push.

On the back of this extraordinary success, Waterman produced his masterstroke. Although both Kylie and Jason Donovan had long since left Neighbours to pursue their singing careers, the transmission time delay meant that their two characters were still in the cast in the UK. Consequently when the Neighbours scriptwriters decided that Charlene and Scott should get married, the ensuing furore made it one of the social events of the year and sent the Kylie-Jason romance rumours into overdrive. Waterman decided it was time to crank up the action, and did so with the syrupy duet 'Especially For

You' which convinced the nation that a real marriage was imminent.

The success of the single marked a watershed in Kylie and Jason's career. For some reason it had been assumed that it would be Donovan who would supersede Kylie's initial bubblegum success and go on to carve out a long-lasting pop career – especially when, in 1989, Kylie followed the time-honoured route into movies with a lead role in the indifferently received The Delinquents.

Kylie's army of fans had different ideas, however, and her subsequent single and album releases continued to be snapped up. Jason's singing career, by contrast, was suffocated by litigation arising out of a magazine article claiming he was gay. He wasn't, but the lengthy court proceedings left him exhausted and disillusioned and with the beginnings of a drug habit that would continue into the 1990s. He would reappear in the mid-1990s as a stage star in the highly rated production of Joseph And The Amazing Technicolour Dreamcoat, but he was no longer the fresh-faced teen idol of just a few years earlier.

Kylie, meanwhile, would plod through the 1990s with a string of unremarkable singles until, at the end of the decade, she reinvented herself spectacularly with the Cathy Dennis-penned 'Can't Get You Out Of My Head'. The single shot to the top of the charts on the back of an irresistible dance rhythm and a change of image that saw tomboy Charlene transformed into a sexy vamp whose rear end became one of the most talked-about pieces of real estate of the new millennium.

crap, and I know they are, because I've been there 20 times before... I'll just let 'em get on with it and then shout "Next!"'

Still, it did not stop Waterman from instigating his own Parnes-style roadshows showcasing new SAW acts. And, he admitted at the time, 'If we ever have an argument about who is top of the bill, I say, "Wait a minute, I've got to tell you that it says over the top of the band, 'Pete Waterman's roadshow – The Hitman Roadshow.'" So I'm the fucking star, right? I'm the one that's on the TV *every* week. I'm the one that's put this together, got the sponsorship. I'm always right.'

When the SAW team went on stage to receive a prestigious music industry award in the late 1980s, they were roundly booed by industry figures, who regarded them as little more than bubblegum manufacturers. But the primary motive was jealousy. Even their detractors found it difficult to argue with the extent of SAW's power. At its peak, it seemed Waterman had only to point his finger and some lucky youngster would be turned into an overnight pop sensation with a song dashed off by Stock and Aitken. Sonia, Big Fun and Brother Beyond all enjoyed their 15 minutes of fame after being sprinkled with SAW gold dust. Donna Summer briefly rekindled her flagging career courtesy of SAW, while their greatest triumph was without doubt transforming a pair of D-list Australian soap stars into Kylie and Jason, the biggest pop acts of the decade.

Pete Waterman: self-pronounced Hit Man who nevertheless lived up to his grand title by discovering a string of '80s pop starlets

Frankie Says: Trevor, Paul And The Band Of The Decade

One of the men behind one of the most audacious marketing phenomena of the 1980s was, ironically, the man who had just a couple of years earlier foretold the death of the radio star at the hands of video. If the Buggles had been formed by producer Trevor Horn in order to get his message across, then Frankie Goes To Hollywood was proof that he practised what he preached.

Frankie's lead singer Holly Johnson maintains that the group and their startling début single 'Relax' were already in existence before Horn and his co-conspirator Paul Morley set to work. 'Paul Morley had such an ego he wanted to make out he'd created us. But when he first met us we were already called Frankie Goes To Hollywood, and we'd done the song on a John Peel radio session. The words were exactly the same, the bassline, the beat, the groove, were all exactly the same.'

Johnson is right. But the original recording of 'Relax' is almost unrecognisable from the masterpiece of production that Horn manufactured. The influential Peel played it, but nobody bought it.
Even so, the Frankies had another more pressing career problem that Johnson hints at when he says, 'We had this outrageous stage act which all the record labels thought was too hot to handle.'

In fact, the stage act – which took the form of a leather-clad orgy at a gay S&M club – was so explicit that it rendered the band untenable. Gay might have been the new Straight in the sexually tolerant 1980s, but there were still limits to what the general public would tolerate.

Paul Morley was an acerbic British rock journalist who knew enough about the machinations of the industry to encourage him to conduct his own experiment in manufactured pop. His starting point was the curious paradox that, although homosexuality had always been rife in the music business, almost every gay artist did their damnedest to keep their sexuality a secret. Even at the beginning of the 1980s, gender benders like Boy George preferred to play a game of hide-and-seek with the press – witness his 'I prefer a nice cup of tea to sex' statement – rather than openly admit the fact that they were gay. Morley's brainwave was to market a group who were not, in the words of Simon Napier-Bell, the 'limp-wristed jolly boys the British public so loved', but were aggressive and upfront about their homosexuality. His investigations soon led him to Liverpool, where Holly Johnson and his partner Paul Rutherford fitted the bill perfectly.

Morley had by now teamed up with Trevor Horn, who had once been the lead singer of Yes but who, after his success with the Buggles, had retreated behind a mixing desk. They both decided that, while Frankie Goes To Hollywood's stage act was beyond the pale, 'Relax' had tremendous outrage potential. The song, essentially, was a manual of controlled ejaculation – but the lyrics were sufficiently ambiguous ('Shoot me with your laser beams') to pass for the usual pop nonsense, while still maintaining enough pointed references ('Relax don't do it, when you want to come') to excite the chattering classes.

Frankie Goes To Hollywood, fronted by Holly Johnson, made the fatal but inevitable mistake of believing their own hype

announced on air that 'Relax' was a disgusting record and succeeded in getting it banned by the BBC. Sales inevitably soared, and from that moment on the band could be as open as they liked about their sexuality. Suddenly it was open season on homophobes as gays flooded out of the cupboard. Everybody now had a gay friend and it was no problem, because these were liberal times and the BBC and white, middle-aged gay-bashers like Mike Read were a disgrace.

The BBC relented and 'Relax' was restored to Radio 1's play-list – but the damage had already been done. By acting as a self-appointed arbiter of musical decency, Read had adminstered a self-inflicted credibility blow from which he, Dave Lee 'Hairy Cornflake' Travis, Noel 'Noelie' Edmonds, Simon 'Simes' Bates and others in Radio One's aged DJ autocracy would never recover. Within ten years most of them would be farmed out to obscure Gold stations, their protests drowned out by the relentless jabber of presenters young enough to be their grandchildren.

The Frankies weren't the only beneficiaries of the BBC's blunder. Since 1981, Tyne Tees Television, a commercial TV outpost in Newcastle upon Tyne, had been broadcasting The Tube to the nation. An often-shambolic 90-minute live music show which featured all of the top acts and introduced dozens more, it had already supplanted BBC's Top Of The Pops and The Old Grey Whistle Test as Britain's number one pop show. When Morley announced that the Frankies' next single, 'Two Tribes', would be accompanied by a spectacular and unforgettable video and that its world premiere was to be on *The Tube*, the show got its highest ever ratings and the BBC got a painful bloody nose.

For once, Morley's hype was justified. The ten-minute 'Two Tribes' video, made by promo pioneers and former 10cc members Godley and Creme, featured caricatures of US President Reagan and Soviet leader Chernenko knocking seven bells out of each other in a wrestling ring. It was supposed to symbolise the worrying Cold War nuclear arms proliferation of the time, as was the song itself, with its chilling air-raid siren intro and actor Patrick Allen's grim narration lifted from government instructions on what to do in the event of a nuclear attack. 'Two Tribes' found Trevor Horn at the top of his game, and it surpassed 'Relax' by remaining at the top of the charts for nine weeks.

Trevor Horn: production genius who gave Frankie Goes To Hollywood their distinctive sound in the 1980s

El DeBarge from DeBarge: the group looked uncannily like The Jacksons – but that was where the similarities ended

DeBarge

Pop fans have always shown a peculiar fondness for family-based groups, so it is just as well that there has always been a steady stream of all-singing, all-dancing families to satisfy their craving. But while some, like The Osmonds and the Jackson 5, have become legends, others... well, others haven't quite made it into the same neighbourhood.

There were great hopes for the DeBarge family in the early 1980s, especially among Motown executives, who had plucked the four brothers and one sister from the obscurity of Grand Rapids, Michigan, and groomed them to be the natural successors of the Jackson 5. But the reasoning behind this strategy was also its most obvious flaw: lead singer El DeBarge looked uncannily like Michael Jackson – but that was where the similarities between the two broods ended.

Still, this didn't stop the marketing department at Motown spending two years grooming the group in preparation for their 1981 début album, *The DeBarges*, which, on the back of a huge publicity campaign, garnered reasonable chart success and established them as a player in the teenybop market. Wider success, however, continued to evade the group, especially in the UK, where they remained resolutely unheard of.

Their big break came in 1985. Michael Jackson had released *Thriller* to extraordinary global acclaim, and his new look – long, oiled hair, half-mast trousers, rolled-up jacket sleeves, and nifty dance routines – was suddenly de rigueur among black artists on both sides of the Atlantic. Motown quickly sent DeBarge for a makeover and, armed with the catchy single 'Rhythm Of The Night', launched them on another global assault. With El now looking even more of a dead ringer for Jacko, even down to the dance routines, the band finally caught on in the UK and the single made the Top 10. Unfortunately, in early 1986 El decided to take the comparison between himself and Jacko one step further and announced that he was leaving his siblings to go solo. His career inevitably nose-dived, as did those of the others. Proof of their fall from grace was provided in 1986, when (just a few short months after their biggest hit) Motown were desperately plugging a DeBarge greatest hits album.

Bros asked when they would be famous – but the question should have been how long? Answer: five minutes

Bros

It was strangely satisfying for men of a certain age to see a recent newspaper photograph of two balding, middle-aged men and realise that they were, in fact, 1980s teen idols Luke and Matt Goss. Similarly cheering was the attendant story that Luke and Matt had got together for a Bros reunion, but been forced to refund the half-dozen people who turned up to see them.

Time is a great leveller, but rampant jealousy takes a great deal of soothing. In the late 1980s, the golden Goss bros captured the hearts of a generation of teenage girls and filled their boyfriends with a simmering hatred. Bros were easy to hate, however: not only were they blond, toned and blessed with movie-star looks, but they exuded an unbearable vanity that was only partly the invention of their bombastic manager Tom Watkins.

Watkins had written Bros's breakthrough hit 'When Will I Be Famous' when he himself had harboured ambitions of stardom. When that came to nothing, he found the Goss brothers to sing it for him. He couldn't have chosen better. Before hooking up with Watkins – who was managing the Pet Shop Boys at the time – Luke, Matt and their pal Craig Logan had been pop wannabes desperate for a crack at superstardom at any price.

Watkins gave them what they wanted in spades, ruthlessly marketing them for the teeny audience who, in turn, responded with screaming approval. In 1988, the group slipped easily into the vacuum created by the demise of Wham!, although they preferred socks to shuttlecocks down the front of their jeans. Yet Bros never recaptured the carefree *joie de vivre* of Wham! and at times their in-yer-face ambition made them appear like George and Andrew's little brothers, petulant about having been made to wait their turn in the spotlight.

It was strange also that, while Matt and Luke were twins, the group somehow seemed to play down this most marketable of facts. It would have seemed entirely logical to ditch Craig at the outset and simply have the Goss brothers out front, like teenage Everlys. This would certainly have prevented the seismic falling-out which marked Bros's demise. Instead, they persisted with the façade that they were actually a band, with Matt singing, Luke playing the drums and Craig on the bass.

Still, the line-up didn't affect their sales. 'When Will I Be Famous' was followed by a string of Top 10 hits, including 'I Owe You Nothing', 'I Quit', 'Cat Among The Pigeons' and 'Too Much'.

The adulation for Matt and Luke was certainly too much for Craig, who found himself lampooned as 'the other one', or even 'Derek', whenever the band were discussed. Pondering whether or not to leave the band, in early 1989 the decision was taken for him and he was kicked out... although he didn't go without a fight. The subsequent bitter legal battle with Watkins derailed the band as it was travelling at full speed, and the carnage was terrible to behold. It was two years before Matt and Luke were back in the charts, this time sporting a more mature image. But their goose had long been cooked and the loyal army of girl fans who had made them the toast of 1988 had moved on. In 1993, the brothers split as an act, with Luke turning to acting and Matt to a solo career, but the inevitable oblivion beckoned. They resurfaced in the late 1990s for an ill-fated reunion, but today their aged faces are pin-ups only for the boyfriends who hated them with such a passion 15 years ago

Salutary lesson: Hear'Say were created by the public and swiftly destroyed by it

5

Pop has indeed eaten itself

1990s...

There was a quiet desperation about the so-called Britpop movement of the 1990s, something inherently Canute-ish about the way it stood against the tidal wave of American street culture sweeping relentlessly across the Atlantic, and the frenetic manufacturing of bubblegum pop both in the US and the UK.

By reviving the tradition of earthy, working-class guitar bands, and even hyping an updated Beatles versus Stones clash in the form of Blur versus Oasis, the British music establishment believed it could once again rule the waves by summoning the spirit of the 1960s. But the cold truth was that, while Liam Gallagher's foul mouth and Damon Albarn's middle-class erudition made for good headlines, the majority of British kids couldn't give two hoots for either them or their music. Their heroes were black New York rappers, house music DJs, and a raft of bubblegum pop groups specifically manufactured to satisfy their requirements.

Taking The Rap

The origins of rap music are said to have been in DJs talking over instrumental tracks at New York nightclubs in the 1970s. This explanation sounds plausible enough, although (with all things in the music world) there will be other people who believe other things.

In any case, by 1990 rap and hiphop music had spread like a rash to become the lingua franca not only of Uzi-toting ghetto gangstas from the Bronx, but of wannabe teenies from Arkansas to Aldershot who lapped up the look and the in yer face aggression of leading rappers such as Ice-T, Snoop Doggy Dog and Niggaz With Attitude. But, despite its global appeal, street music was always an American phenomenon, for the simple reason that its terminology and sentiments only sounded convincing when uttered in a booming American accent. Brits were as infatuated with guttural US rap as the Yanks had been with the Liverpool twang 30 years earlier. As a result, it opened the floodgates for a wave of US acts to swamp the UK.

Of course, 'genuine' rap tended to contain references to cop-killing, drug-taking, and slapping up bitches and 'ho's. It was also liberally smattered with the word 'muthafucka'. As a result, a sanitised version was required for wider consumption, which was perfect for bubblegum record producers and managers anxious to cash in on the rapping and hiphop trend.

Leading the first wave in the 1990s were New Kids On The Block, whose brand of ersatz rapping and macho posturing had been created by Maurice Starr at the back end of the 1980s. Their debut Number 1 in the UK was 'Hangin' Tough', which contained as much black street slang and attitude as it was possible for five well-to-do white boys from Boston to reproduce for a family audience. It was a

New Kids On The Block were middle-class white boys who were told to hang tough and became chart-topping megastars in the US and the UK

formula that had already proved phenomenally successful in the US, where their first nine singles had reached the Top 10. The conquest of Britain in 1990 raised their profile even further, and by the end of the year – thanks to the relentless flogging of such merchandise as cartoons, comics, dolls and videos – the New Kids had netted nearly $100 million (£65 million) and were in *Fortune* magazine's Top 10 of entertainment earners.

Boyz II Men

By the time New Kids On The Block's requisite 18 months of fame were almost up, they had been supplanted in teenie affections by Boyz II Men, four black boys from Philadelphia who had taken the precaution of naming themselves after one of the New Kids' early hits.

Consisting of Wanya 'Squirt' Morris, Michael 'Bass' McCary, Shawn 'Slim' Stockman and Nathan 'Alex-Vanderpool' Morris, the four had met at Philadelphia's High School of Creative and Performing Arts in 1988. Modelling themselves closely on the harmless posturing, rapping and close harmonies of the New Kids, they won a talent show in front of their fellow students, and it was this that brought them to the attention of Michael Bivins, a former member of 1980s boy band New Edition.

Bivins immediately saw that Boyz II Men fitted the immediate requirements of a teen market already primed by the New Kids, and quickly negotiated a recording deal with Motown. In 1991, their début album *Cooleyhighharmony* was released to great acclaim, not least because of the cunning way in which one side of the album consisted of dance music and the other side ballads, thereby ensuring wide-ranging airplay and garnering a remarkable five million sales worldwide.

Their lasting memory, however, was the song 'End Of The Road', which was culled from the Eddie Murphy movie *Boomerang* and which spent a mammoth 11 weeks at the top of the US charts and three at Number 1 in the UK. Because of this unprecedented success, the Boyz largely dropped the dance routines and concentrated instead on cheesy ballads. Again it was a shrewd move, as through to 1994 they racked up a succession of hits both in the US and the UK, becoming at the same time one of the biggest-selling bands of all time.

At the end of 1994 they decided to take a break, presumably to spend their money, since the hiatus would last three years. When they returned, they found themselves in a pop world almost exclusively populated by boy bands in which they were now just aged also-rans. An album, *Nathan Michael Shawn Wanya*, was studiously ignored by a new teenybopper audience and the Boyz had, like so many superstars before them, discovered that the only constant of bubblegum pop was its fickleness.

Four Hunks And A Fat One Who Writes The Songs: The Rise Of Take That

It was only a matter of time before the British music industry got its act in gear and started churning out manufactured pop bands like it had always done, but in the 1990s there was a mysterious reticence about doing so that lasted almost to the middle of the decade.

Perhaps it was a hangover from Stock, Aitken and Waterman's unprecedented success in the 1980s. The partnership had broken up at the beginning of the 1990s, but its influence still hung heavy over the UK industry: there was a feeling that kids were overdosed on saccharine, formula pop, and the success of the more streetwise American acts did nothing to dispel this opinion. (There was also, of course, the fact that Britain had no convincing answer to the US hiphop and rap acts.)

Salvation came in the gradual mutation of New Kids and Boyz II Men from street warriors to sweet-voiced balladeers. Now ballads were something that the Brits *could* do.

Nigel Martin-Smith was a gay entertainment agency boss from Manchester who, in 1991, saw the success of the raunchy American boy bands and decided to go out and create his own. The result was Take That, who garnered a few headlines with their début single 'Do What U Like' largely because of a risqué video sequence showing the band members' bare buttocks. Subsequent singles bombed, however, and by 1993 it looked like the band would remain an insignificant footnote even among the rubble of here today, gone tomorrow bubblegum popsters.

'He [Martin-Smith] thinks he knows what talent is,' crowed the old hitmeister Pete Waterman. 'Nigel Martin-Smith is nice to people because he doesn't know whether they are good or bad.'

But Waterman was wrong. Martin-Smith had in fact created the ideal boy band. It was just that, before 1993, they were trying to be something that they quite patently weren't. If their lead singer had come from the Bronx, they might have got away with it. But he wasn't. He was from Frodsham.

Gary Barlow was a prodigious and talented songwriter who, as a teenager, had formed a band called The Cutest Rush with his Manchester pal Mark Owen. Martin-Smith knew of the band and, when it came to creating his own, he recruited Barlow and Owen as the musical nucleus. But the manager also knew that musical talent was only one part of the jigsaw. Whatever his other talents, Barlow was always moon-faced and tubby-looking. To make matters worse for a boy band, he couldn't dance to save his life. He recalled, 'Whenever those teenage magazines came out with a poll on their readers' favourite member, I always came in an embarrassing fifth. And I always found concerts difficult because I'm an awful dancer.' Owen, meanwhile, was good-looking but lacking in dynamism. Many managers would have simply ditched Barlow and got in a good-looking beefcake to make up the numbers. But Martin-Smith was canny enough to realise that a boy band needed at least someone who could hold a tune.

The solution to his problem was Howard Donald and Jason Orange, a couple of likely lads from nearby Droylsden who had formed a breakdancing duo called Street Beat. Possessed of negligible musical ability, they nevertheless added the vital spring-heeled ingredient into the mix. What was lacking, Martin-Smith now realised, was personality. Fortunately, he had just the man on his books, a would-be actor from Stoke called Robbie Williams, whose dad had been a cabaret entertainer. After Williams performed a rendition of 'Any Dream Will Do' (The Joseph song recently revived in the charts by 1980s pop idol Jason Donovan), he was accepted with open arms into the band.

'When you looked at Take That, it was impossible to imagine that they hadn't been friends forever,' says the journalist Charlotte Raven. 'The idea of Jason and Mark being picked up from different street corners just wouldn't have fitted the picture. If anything, they looked more like old mates than old mates ever could have – a tribute to Take That supremo Nigel Martin-Smith, whose genius was to understand that the whole point of a manufactured band was to distil what everyone liked about real ones and magnify it to the power of ten.'

Yet, under Martin-Smith's guidance, it still took Take That the best part of two years to achieve any meaningful chart success. Then they dropped the macho bullshit and things started to happen. Their cover version of the Tavares single 'It Only Takes A Minute' got to Number 7, at which point the British tabloids, anxiously sniffing for some home-grown bubblegum to rival the Americans, fell on them like grateful hounds.

The resulting teen frenzy rivalled anything that had been seen before. As Barlow recalls, 'For three years, we basically ruled Europe. Take That broke records and won endless awards, and we sold about ten million albums. At each of our concerts, we'd sell £100,000 [approximately $150,000] worth of merchandise a night. Take That was a moneymaking machine.'

Ironically, one of the key factors in Take That's success was the emergence of Barlow himself as a songwriter of universal appeal. Uncomfortable and unconvincing in the spotlight – especially live on stage – Barlow instead retreated behind his piano, and the results were sensational. Songs like 'Pray' (an Ivor Novello Award winner) and 'A Million Love Songs' (written originally when he was just 16) captured the hearts, not only of the teenyboppers, but of their mothers too. 'Back For Good' is probably as good a song as any released in the 1990s, and saw the band finally crack the US market in the middle of 1995.

Something for everybody: in many ways Take That were the perfect boy band

But, as ever, the end was lurking round the next corner. In Take That's case, the catalyst was the troubled Robbie Williams who by 1995 had become fed up of the bubblegum treadmill. 'The band had the creativity of mentally unstable morons and was spawned by Satan,' Williams said later. 'The manager Nigel Martin-Smith really mucked me up emotionally. He managed me and manipulated me from when I was 16. It was the devil's pact – he gave you fame and riches, you gave him your soul and 25 per cent of the takings.'

Even the usually taciturn Barlow admitted that, after four years, the life of a teen idol was becoming hard to stomach. 'It was unbearable. To get inside my house, I'd have to get the police to move everyone. Then the phone would ring, and it would be a fan who'd got hold of my number. It was just horrible going home. It was no joke.'

Barlow and the rest of the band also found it increasingly difficult to live up to the goody-two-shoes image that had been created for them by Martin-Smith. 'The official Take That line was always, "We don't have relationships". Full stop. Of course, everybody did, and it was tremendously hard to keep under wraps. All the English newspapers were on our back day and night. Sneaking people into hotel rooms was horrible, it really was.'

When Williams inevitably left to go solo, it was only a matter of time before the rest of Take That followed suit. To their credit, they did so with a certain amount of élan – certainly more than Williams had shown during his ill-tempered departure. Their cover version of the old Bee Gees hit 'How Deep Is Your Love' zoomed straight to the top, leaving their army of fans weeping into their hankies but with fond memories to keep them going.

It was, naturally, the talented Barlow who most people expected to carve out a successful solo career. Curiously, the affable Take That frontman bombed almost immediately, failing to trouble even the furthest reaches of the charts with his foot-tapping output. It was left to Robbie Williams to make the grade as a solo performer, emerging from a self-inflicted period of booze and drug abuse with a string of Top 10 hits. His reward in 2003 was an £80 million contract from EMI. However, the inflated advance was based on the assumption that he would be able to crack the American market. So far he has failed to do so, and with his recent slump in chart success, it could be that his meteor has already reached its zenith.

Spiceworld

In 1985, a nerdy-looking synthesiser player called Paul Hardcastle got to the top of the charts with a catchy tune called '19', about the Vietnam War. His manager was called Simon Fuller. It was Fuller's first taste of pop's big time and within 15 years he would be one of the most powerful men in the music industry, having not only exploited it quite brilliantly by creating one of manufactured pop's biggest names, but having changed the face of pop music irrevocably.

The Spice Girls have always made a great deal of the fact that it was they, not Fuller, who first formed the group. That is true enough. Melanie Brown, Melanie Chisholm, Geri Halliwell, Emma Bunton and Victoria Adams had met on several occasions, mostly at failed auditions for film and dance jobs. In 1993, they were living together in a house in Berkshire, toying with the idea of forming a pop group but with little idea of how to go about it.

Fuller was also toying with the idea of forming a pop group, and the five ordinary-looking girls who were brought to his attention in

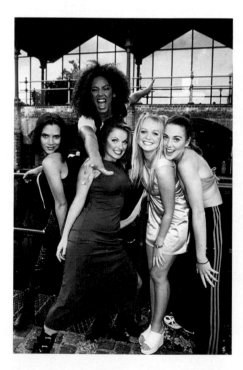

The Spice Girls were not so much a pop group as a global marketing phenomenon

Peter Andre: six-pack superstar in Australia; standing joke everywhere else

Peter Andre

'Since they know I don't do drugs, that I'm faithful, that I take care of my body, they have nothing to go on and have to resort to sarcasm,' whined Peter Andre back in 1995. His bitterness was understandable. Since coming to the UK a year earlier from Australia, where he had established himself as a leading teen idol, Andre had found himself subjected to a barrage of hilarity.

This too was understandable. With his sculpted six-pack stomach, flawless skin and glazed expression, Andre resembled a store dummy – which was ironic, because after his first two UK singles failed to trouble the Top 40, he found himself performing with other bubblegum wannabes on an endless round of shopping-centre roadshows.

His singular lack of success and the relentless scorn that was heaped on him must have made the UK seem a far cry from Oz. There, he had not only been asked to support both Bobby Brown and Madonna on their Australian tours, but ended 1993 by sweeping the board at the Australian Music Awards, winning Best New Act, Best New Dance Act and Highest Selling Single for 'Gimme Little Sign'.

Maybe it was just that the British record-buying public weren't going to be fooled by every bubblegum popster who was dangled before them in the 1990s. Maybe it was that Andre took himself far too seriously. 'My songs are either about experiences I've had, or experiences that other people have had, or experiences that I wish I've had', was just one of his typically inane pearls as he did the rounds of Saturday-morning kids' shows in his bid to be recognised.
It would not be until March 1996 that Andre would taste anything like success, when his single 'Only One' got to Number 16 in the UK chart. After that, he finally got to Number 1 with 'Mysterious Girl' and then 'Flava', which earned the dubious distinction of knocking the Spice Girls off the top. Only the most heartless cynic would deny Andre his moment of glory after all his effort, and it would be nice to say he remained at the top for the next ten years. Sadly, within a year he had largely been forgotten, although not in the Far East, where he remains a well-known celebrity to this day.

1995 were precisely what he was looking for. He signed them up and then set in motion a campaign that was almost military in its precision.

'I consciously, methodically did my homework for weeks,' he said of the long hours during which he studied the pop charts on both sides of the Atlantic and formulated his plan. One thing that struck him clearly was that, while boy bands were now all the rage, with Take That and Boyzone leading the way in the UK, there was no female equivalent. Other managers would simply have put Geri and co in some skimpy frocks and sent them straight out with a Supremes cover version, but Fuller was acutely aware that, for his group to survive, they needed a gimmick.

Thus Girl Power was born.

Rock historian Colin Larkin sums up the basic idea when he says, 'They [the Spice Girls] managed to add post-feminist attitude to a commercial pop package – the boys could still fancy them, although their first loyalty was to each other and their fellow females.'

It was, of course, utter hokum. While Geri was spouting such nonsense as 'You [men] can be masculine as well, same as Girl Power goes with femininity. But if you're a boy, don't pretend to be anything else' and, even better, 'It's very desettling [sic] for male dominated newspapers to realise that five women in short skirts have got a brain on them', Fuller was frantically signing sponsorship and advertising deals with Pepsi, Walkers, Impulse, Asda, Polaroid, Cadbury's, Unilever, Sony and Chupa Chups sweets.

When quizzed about this, Sporty Spice memorably said, 'We believe in everything we endorse. I like crisps.'

Crucial to the success was the image that Fuller created for his charges. With their carefully crafted and largely bogus personas, 'Posh', 'Baby', 'Sporty', 'Ginger' and 'Scary' were a ready-made merchandising range guaranteed to appeal to the pre-pubescent girls who made up the bulk of their fanbase. Their first hit, 'Wannabe', supposedly espoused Girl Power philosophy, although it was anyone's guess what the chorus line 'zigazig-ha!' had to do with the concept. Nevertheless, the kids bought into the idea right from the beginning and sent the single straight to the top of the charts. The subsequent album, *Spice*, contained ten tracks plus an application to join the Spice Girl Squad, which entitled fans to a Spice Girls ID card and the group's newsletter, both of which were guaranteed to give them 'Instant Girl Power!'

All the while, the girls did their stuff by coming out with cod philosophy to anyone who would listen. 'Yeah, drop all the macho stuff,' Scary advised her male fans. 'It's nice to have a conversation with a man without beady eyes where they shouldn't be. Platonic, like.'

By the end of 1997, the Spice Girls had two multimillion–selling albums, a film called Spiceworld, a 200-item merchandise catalogue, half a dozen slickly crafted videos and enough momentum for any TV station confidently to give them a substantial amount of air time.

Larry LeBlanc of Billboard magazine correctly identified the root of the phenomenon when he said in 1997, 'The thing that has happened in the last two or three years is that record company people have woken up and said, "Wait a minute, we have not been servicing the eight- to 12 year-old marketplace". What you're talking about really is an awakening of essentially an audience that was disenfranchised about ten years ago as all the companies ran off and tried to sign grunge bands.'

But while the market in 8-year-olds on both sides of the Atlantic had largely been conquered within the first few months of the Spice Girls' existence, the quintet still had enough tricks up their sleeves to keep the adults – in the form of the tabloids – interested in their activities. Many of the headlines were generated by Ginger Spice.

First, Ginger's past life as a topless model somewhat belatedly hit the front pages. This was followed by an interview in the upmarket Spectator magazine in which both she and Posh claimed to be supporters of Conservative Prime Minister John Major (as opposed to the hordes of pop stars who would soon clamour to be associated with Tony Blair and New Labour). Next came the surprise ditching of Simon Fuller, the man who had secured them 21 million record sales as well as millions of pounds in their bank accounts.

The reasons for the split were never fully explained, although it was widely rumoured at the time that Ginger was the instigator. At the time, the girls complained of being tired because of their punishing work schedules and also that they wanted to have more control over their destiny. However, Fuller's sacking came just as the Spice Girls launched the Poppy Appeal with Dame Vera Lynn, shared a photo call with Nelson Mandela and the Prince of Wales in South Africa, and were voted Best Band in the World at the MTV Awards. It was difficult to see how much more popular they could be, even if they were pulling their own strings.

Pete Waterman identified the age-old problem when he said, 'There is a point in every artist's career when they start to believe their own publicity. This is when the danger signs start and [for the Spice Girls] the red light has just come on.' Fuller didn't mind. He was already hatching even more ambitious plans, of which we will see more later.

As for the Spice Girls…well, the relaxation of their punishing schedule effectively meant their expansion into more leisurely solo careers. The

London's version of ghetto hiphop came courtesy of East 17 – but not for long

inevitable was hastened by the departure of Ginger, who at first looked like being the most successful solo Spice of the lot. With her new slimline appearance, she charted with a couple of catchy singles, then baled out to the safety of fitness videos and TV appearances before the public realised she couldn't sing.

Posh had already taken the precaution of marrying footballer David Beckham and thus becoming one half of the celebrity couple of the decade, Britain's unofficial royal family. Unfortunately, this did not stop her singing ambitions – but after a series of atonal flops these were stopped for her when she was dumped by her record company.

Mel B flirted only briefly with singing, but gained more fame outside the group by her ill-fated marriage to Dutch dancer Jimmy Gulzar and the birth of a child.

Poor Emma Bunton seemed destined for oblivion, also being dumped by her record company despite three Top 5 hits, until (in May 2003) she struck a lucrative deal with none other than Simon Fuller. This only further fuelled persistent rumours that the pair had been having an affair all along.

It was left to Mel C to develop into a genuine solo artist. Casting off her tracksuit, she unleashed the album *Northern Star* which, while never as commercial as the offerings from her Spice Girl chums, was by far the most critically acclaimed.

The Spice Girls, whatever one's personal taste, were an example of manufactured pop at its finest: a winning concept brilliantly realised,

East 17

East 17, from the Walthamstow district of east London whence they took their name, were a prime example of why white English boys shouldn't do hard-core rap and hiphop.

It wasn't really their fault. Signed up by former Bros manager, the ebullient Tom Watkins, the group were cynically moulded into Bronx-style homeboys, complete with ill-fitting jeans, reversed baseball caps and devil's head hand signals. Quite rightly, they were immediately scoffed at by critics upon their arrival on the scene in 1992, although in retrospect the two lead members of the group, Brian Harvey and Tony Mortimer, would prove good value for money in the bad-behaviour stakes.

East 17's early success allowed them to lift a finger to their detractors. Their début single 'House Of Love' got to the Top 10 and 'Deep' reached the Top 5. There then followed a wobbly period in which the band made more headlines from groping female journalists and farting in public than from their records, but late 1994 saw them back with a vengeance with the Number 1 smash 'Stay Another Day'.

It was noticeable, however, that this hit – a cheesy orchestral ballad – maintained the band's marked change from New York hiphop into more mainstream and commercially viable Take That territory.

It was to prove their finest moment. One thing that had become clear during East 17's brief career to date was the growing songwriting ability of Tony Mortimer. On the eve of a triumphal tour in 1995, Mortimer collapsed with exhaustion and the band fell apart in disarray. Brian Harvey, in particular, began to live life as if he was a Bronx rapper, but his bragging about drugs backfired when he was sacked from the band for lauding ecstasy. By then Mortimer had left, and the band was effectively over.

Harvey's attempt to relaunch it as E-17 almost came off when their single 'Each Time' got to Number 2 in 1998, but subsequent releases bombed. Harvey continues to attempt comebacks, but few are holding their breath.

willing band members prepared to play the game, marketing of the highest order and self-publicity so good that eventually the band members believed it themselves. In many people's eyes, the Spices were *the* band of the 1990s – and it is difficult to argue. While Oasis and Blur fought their contrived Britpop battle, it was the Spice Girls who dominated the charts and the headlines, the Spice Girls who conquered America, the Spice Girls who were in fact what the rest of the world outside the UK recognised as 'Britpop'.

Their success had little to do with their music, which (apart from 'Wannabe) was largely forgettable. It had a great deal to do with the girls themselves, who, while Liam Gallagher was making an arse of himself on Oasis's abortive sorties to America, were smiling, keeping to the script and winning over US audiences in the same way The Beatles had more than 30 years before.

But what made the Spice Girls special above all was the concept so carefully constructed by Simon Fuller – Svengali Spice, as he became known – a man so well versed in the mechanics of bubblegum pop that even Pete Waterman gave him grudging praise. And, now that he had proved what he could do, Fuller was about to take the concept to its natural conclusion.

Gangsta's Paradise?

How one perceives American pop in the 1990s is very much down to what one thinks of gangsta rap, because for long, turgid periods of the decade the *Billboard* chart appeared to have been transformed into a New York ghetto populated exclusively by angry young black men with initials for names and venom on their tongues.

Tupac Shakur, or 2Pac, was typical of them. The son of two Black Panther members (his mother was pregnant with him while she was in jail), his musical career became an occasional interlude between jail sentences and gang feuds and was ended in 1996 when he was gunned down in Las Vegas.

The alternative to the rappers was often just as bad. Ageing divas like Mariah Carey and Whitney Houston spent the decade performing increasingly self-indulgent vocal gymnastics, while names like Jacko, Elton and Celine clung onto the Top 10 like decrepit limpets. Grunge, in the form of bands like Nirvana, was a viable white alternative to rap but, like its homeboy equivalent, it was a brand of music that either grabbed or alienated.

In such a climate, it is no surprise that bubblegum bands like Boyz II Men were able to make such an impact on the US charts, scoring three of the best-selling singles in American chart history. And no surprise, either, that other young and eager boy bands followed in their wake, desperate to cash in on the lucrative (mainly female teeny) market that the rappers, the divas, grungers and limpets had left exposed.

Hanson

With the US charts increasingly dominated by the likes of 2Pac preaching sentiments like 'United we stand, divided we fall, they can shoot one nigga but they can't shoot us all', Middle America felt it was high time it fought back. It did so the only way it knew how: with good ol' family entertainment.

Thus, in 1997, the Hanson family sprang forth from Tulsa, Oklahoma, and for a few blissful months filled in the gap between the years of gangsta rap and those of Britney Spears.

There were three Hansons, the eldest being 17 years old and the youngest, the drummer Zac, barely 12. To be fair to them, they were a talented trio who had been around for a number of years (at least, since Zac was 6). But with the *Billboard* pop chart virtually a closed shop for rappers from New York and Boyz II Men, Hanson spent much of the 1990s being rejected by record companies, who saw no future in renascent Osmonds.

Their success came thanks to the perseverance of their manager Chris Sabec, who finally secured them a contract with Mercury Records. At this point the obvious and most well-trodden route would have been to dress the boys up in matching suits and focus all the attention on little Zac – at least until his voice broke. Instead Sabec and his team took the bold step of marketing Hanson as a sort of milk-toothed Nirvana, complete with grungy look and long hair.

At first it worked: their début single 'MmmBop!' went to Number 1 in the US and Top 10 in the UK, on the basis of an uncontrollably catchy hook line and the Hanson brothers' cool slacker image. By the end of 1997 they had enjoyed three more transatlantic single hits and best-selling album.

But there, bizarrely, it ended. The band set off on an extensive three-year tour and seemed to forget about releasing singles. All their record-buying fans had to show for their devotion was a horrendous Christmas album called *Snowed In For Christmas* and a half-hearted collection of early material. By the time the boys got back in the studio to record *This Time Around* in 2000, most had voted with their feet: the album bombed and the Hansons all but disappeared off the face of the earth.

5ive

After his success with the Spice Girls, Simon Fuller could have taken five chimpanzees and turned them into overnight bubblegum pop sensations. Instead, he decided to save himself the effort and recruit a boy band who would take a minimal amount of training to get up to speed.

In 1997, more than 3,000 hopefuls turned up to a widely publicised audition held by Fuller and his team, but significantly the five (or rather 5ive) chosen all had extensive stage and music backgrounds. Ritchie Neville and Scott Robinson had been through the National Youth Theatre and Sylvia Young Stage School respectively, Richard Breen was an alumnus of the Italia Conti School, Jason Brown was already working as a DJ, while Sean Conlon was a winner of the Yamaha Young Composer of the Year Award.

His band chosen, Fuller set about moulding them into the finished article, securing lucrative sponsorship deals, and by December of that same year they were in the UK Top 10 with 'Slam Dunk Da Funk'. This was but the prelude to four Top 10 singles the following year, and when one of them, 'When The Lights Go Out', climbed into a similar position in the US chart, Fuller must have been thinking the business was just too easy.

The band's love lives succeeded in keeping the tabloid machine churning, with Neville providing the majority of the column centimetres when he was dating teenage popstar Billie Piper. Then, perhaps inevitably, Neville and Brown told a magazine that they were in favour of legalising cannabis – although, of course, neither admitted smoking it.

Despite the constant publicity, consistent US success would elude them – although neither 5ive nor Simon Fuller was too disappointed. In the UK they had the Number 1 album and single and, when their almost identical version of Queen's 'We Will Rock You' reached the top of the charts in 2001, it seemed they could have released an album of belching and kids would have bought it in their thousands.

Perhaps the band themselves had grown tired of having things their own way when, in September 2001, they announced they were splitting up. 'We've matured and developed massively as a band over the last three and half years and have also grown as individuals,' they said in a statement. 'As the band has got bigger on a global scale, the commitment levels have had to increase and, at times, that has been hard on us all... it really is time to call it a day.

The Backstreet Boys were managed by former New Kids On The Block tour manager Johnny Wright and his wife Donna and, ironically, had been ploughing a moderately successful furrow in Europe before breaking it in their native USA with 'Everybody (Backstreet's Back)'. Originally from Orlando, the Backstreets picked up seamlessly where Boyz II Men had left off, wowing their audiences with a succession of sugary ballads. Their squeaky-clean image was tarnished somewhat when bandmember AJ McClean checked into an alcohol rehabilitation clinic, but in fact it gave them something of an edge in the contrived rivalry that was established between them and fellow Orlando popsters 'N Sync.

Collectively and musically, 'N Sync are barely worth mentioning. They were an identikit boy band whose pap pop was plugged on a tour of US roller rinks and got into the charts thanks to the usual hordes of lovestruck 8-year-olds. Perceived rivalry with The Backstreet Boys generated more sales, but they were largely interchangeable. Their importance in the story of American bubblegum pop at the end of the 1990s, however, is that they contained two members of a new and chilling dynasty that was about to take over the teen scene as it hurtled screaming into the new millennium.

Westlife: from the people who brought you Boyzone

The Mickey Mouse Club Fights Back

The Mickey Mouse Club had begun back in 1929 when kids got together in local cinemas to watch Disney cartoons and exchange merchandise. But in 1955 Uncle Walt built the Disneyland theme park and, in order to help fund it, he licensed *The Mickey Mouse Club* to ABC, who began screening it nationwide with great success. The format, which continued largely unchanged into the 1990s – save for a period in the mid-1970s when the show was briefly axed – was to have the celebrities of the day cavorting about in front of an audience of juvenile 'Mouseketeers'. The 'M.I.C.K.E.Y' theme song was an anthem sung by generations of kids (and, memorably, in the closing scenes of Stanley Kubrick's Vietnam shocker *Full Metal Jacket*).

The two founder members of 'N Sync were Justin Timberlake and JC Chasez, two extrovert youngsters who, like thousands of others over the years, had found a perfect outlet for their precocity on *The Mickey Mouse Club*. Along with fellow Mouseketeers Britney Spears and Christina Aguilera, the four would emerge as the leading teen idols of the new millennium.

Spears initially was the pick of the bunch, although family and friends who knew her as a brat back in Kentwood, Louisiana, in the 1980s were never in any doubt that she would go all the way. Nor was she.'I love performing,' she said, in a mantra that has accompanied her

Westlife

If it ain't broke, don't fix it. The old saying could be the motto of Irish bubblegum Svengali Louis Walsh, who, after tasting phenomenal success with Boyzone, repeated the formula to the letter with Westlife. Almost everything was a carbon copy, from the two singers/three meatheads make-up to the relentless milking of cheesy cover versions. The only difference was the level of success, which exceeded even that of Ronan and Boyzone.

Not that Ronan cared. He had been brought in as co-manager and producer and was therefore able to smooth the passing of the boy-band baton even further.

The group began when three part-time actors from Sligo – Kian Egan, Shane Filan and Mark Feehily – formed a boy band called IOU with three pals from the locality. Walsh, naturally on the lookout for successors to Boyzone, liked what he saw and signed them up. Changing their name to Westside, ditching the three pals and importing beefcake in the form of Nicky Byrne and Bryan McFadden, he sent them out to support The Backstreet Boys when the US troupe were on tour in Dublin.

There was a brief hiccup when, in a scenario reminiscent of *This Is Spinal Tap*, Walsh discovered that there were about a dozen US boy bands currently called Westside. A slight adjustment in the name and the Westlife juggernaut was up and running again. 'Swear It Again', their début single in May 1999, and 'If I Let You Go', the following August, both topped the charts, and their position was then consolidated with a series of dirge-like cover versions including 'Flying Without Wings', 'I Have A Dream' and 'Against All Odds'. The latter was performed with Mariah Carey, presumably in a bid to conquer the American market (which failed), although by then the UK chart

was like putty in their hands. When 'My Love' reached Number 1 in November 2000, it was their seventh consecutive chart topper, equalling a record set by The Beatles.

Inevitable comparisons between the two bands served to prove that there was no comparison, however. As journalist Darren Waters said, 'Westlife have taken the well-worked formula of the boy band and stripped back any excesses and frills – even Take That had a modicum of raunch and sex appeal – to create a streamlined, marketable product that is easy both on the eye and the ears. The band's musical output is almost entirely made up of non-experimental ballads. The Fab Four may have started out with simple crowd pleasers, such as "Love Me Do", but they soon moved on to songs which redefined the boundaries of pop music.'

A more telling statistic was that, while singles sales in 1999 earned £138 million compared with £14.4 million in 1973, numbers of singles sold were down 22 per cent on the previous year. In other words, bands like Westlife could get to Number 1 by selling a fraction of the number of singles a band like The Beatles sold to reach the same position.

Of course in the end it all came down to marketing, a point rammed home with delicious irony when Westlife were pipped to the Christmas Number 1 slot by a kids' TV character called Bob the Builder.

Shane Filan remained phlegmatic about it. 'I know people still see us as a boy band but I think our music is crossing over,' he said. 'I think you always start off with a young fanbase then reach out to an older audience.'

To prove the point, the band got back to the top with another cover version, this time of Billy Joel's 'Uptown Girl'.

S Club 7: just to prove that Simon Fuller could turn any old dross into a chart-topping act

S Club 7/Steps

When Simon Fuller created 5ive, more than 3,000 turned up to the audition. When he auditioned for S Club 7, there were more than 10,000. The word had clearly got around that being a chart-topping pop star no longer involved slogging round the circuit for years, or playing an instrument, or even showing any previous interest in forming a band. The only inconvenience was that you had to queue up for three hours.

Fuller's idea this time was not simply to create a band but an entire multi-media concept. Getting S Club 7 to the top of the charts was not, he knew, a problem, but what Fuller wanted was total domination of the kiddies market on both sides of the Atlantic. Thus, even as the group were recording their first album, they were already making a *Monkees*–style TV show for broadcast on both US and UK children's television. It worked well enough for a spin-off group S Club Juniors to be pumped out especially for the 4-year-old fans, although by now it was becoming harder and harder even for teenies to find their way through the thicket of identikit groups. One of S Club 7's songs pointedly had a segment in which the band members introduced themselves to each other, just in case they and their fans had forgotten just who the hell they were.

Had the members of S Club and Steps interchanged, only the staunchest of fans could have possibly told the difference. Bleached hair, white teeth, sparkling eyes – and that was just the blokes – the look of each cardboard cut-out was almost identical. It was highly appropriate that the S Club movie, launched to supreme indifference in 2003, featured the band members battling against robot lookalikes. The band members won, but you couldn't tell the difference.

Steps was the creation of Pete Waterman, a money-spinning act of pop cynicism which was more about the Hit Man proving he could still cut it than about any musical statement. Recruited through an advert in *Stage* magazine, the members of the band were a suitable mix of acting-school hopefuls and holiday-camp wannabes, and performed frantic, tightly choreographed insta-pop straight from the Stock, Aitken and Waterman songbook. Even Waterman couldn't take them seriously, describing them as 'Abba on speed'. 'The Archies in human form' would have been a more accurate description.

career. 'I love entertaining. I love to tell stories for people. I think some people are just born to do certain things for people and I'm very lucky and blessed that I knew that this was what I wanted to do.'

The first indication of this came when, barely old enough to walk, she began stealing the spotlight in shows at her local church hall. But, even as a small child, she knew that the quickest way to stardom was to get the hell out of the Deep South.

Her one and only knock-back came when the producer of *The Mickey Mouse Club* told her that, aged just 8, she was too young to become a Mouseketeer. Instead, he put her in touch with an agent in New York, who subsequently got her a place at the Professional Performing Arts Centre. Aged 11, she finally took possession of her coveted black ears and so began two years as a regular on *The Mickey Mouse Club*. Even then, however, Britney had bigger plans.

After making some demo tapes, she was picked up at 16 by Jive Records, whose boss Jeff Fenster later claimed, 'Her vocal ability and commercial appeal caught me right away.'

Fenster immediately set the wheels in motion to make Britney a teen star bar none. And it did not take a genius to work out the angle at which he would play his starlet. Madonna she wasn't; Britney would be portrayed as a God-fearing virgin who loved her mom's apple pie. Except that Fenster, like Malcolm McLaren before him, knew that sex (especially teenage sex) sells. Which is why, when Britney said things like 'I don't believe in sex before marriage. I don't believe in drugs or even smoking. I believe in God', she would appear later that evening on MTV in a skimpy school uniform looking for all the world like a dirty old man's fantasy.

It was Madonna and Debbie Gibson put together in one irre-sistible package, and indeed in interviews Britney admitted her ambi-tion was to follow in the footsteps of Madonna, 'only without all the men, gossip and scandals'.

'If I have on a short skirt it doesn't mean I have low morals,' she said. 'I have very high morals.' And even higher sales.

After a carefully controlled publicity tour of the US, Britney's first single '…Baby One More Time' and her début album of the same name monstered the chart on both sides of the Atlantic. Released in the UK in February 1999, it became one of the fastest-selling singles of all time – shifting 14,000 copies on its first day alone. A bemused Gennaro Castaldo of the HMV chain in London told reporters, 'It's absolutely flying out of the shops. The video is being played heavily on MTV and The Box and that seems to be driving a lot of it.' Explaining the Britney secret, he said, 'She seems to be appealing equally to both sexes. A lot of girls seem to find it aspirational for girls of her age group because they can relate to it. And of course a lot of the guys are into Britney because she's a good-looking girl.'

As Britney's success grew, so did the inevitable tabloid prurience about her sex life, or alleged lack of it. 'When I go home, if I don't make up my bed or wash the dishes – I'm in trouble,' she insisted, but the hacks didn't believe her.

In America the hunt for Britney boyfriends eventually turned up Justin Timberlake, who by then was in 'N Sync and appearing on the same bill as Britney in roadshows organised by teenybopper magazines in the US. The fact that they had been Mouseketeers five years earlier was seen as definitive proof that they were having rampant sex. But, while both eventually coughed to the relationship, both denied it had been consummated.

Cynical oldies in the UK were by now casting their minds back to the 'Are they, aren't they?' Kylie and Jason conundrum so skilfully manufactured by Pete Waterman in the 1980s, and nodding sagely as a new generation of teenies was suckered into believing a wholly unbelievable scenario. In effect, it went all the way back to that famous 'I knew Doris Day *before* she was a virgin' comment. Britney, meanwhile, was appearing half-naked with a snake while still explaining that she was not promoting herself as a sex object. 'I only wear these crop tops because other clothes would make me sweat when I dance,' she said.

The frenzy over Britney and Timberlake ended only when the pair split up, at which point Britney decided to phase out her nice-girl image and try to establish herself as a serious entertainer. Timberlake had no such pretensions. Being in the media spotlight with his fellow former Mouseketeer had the desired effect of springboarding him out of 'N Sync, where he was in danger of being just another part of the wallpaper. He relaunched himself as a solo artist and had immediate transatlantic success.

Mickey Mouse, meanwhile, had unleashed another of his protégés on the pop world. A year older than Britney, and of the same precocious wannabe ilk (she had learned every song from *The Sound of Music* by the age of 5), Christina Aguilera got her ears at the age of 12. 'We were very good friends,' she said of Britney. 'We were the youngest and always looked up to the other kids on the show.'

By the age of 15 she had secured a record contract with RCA, and when she was invited to sing the lead song, 'Reflection', from the Disney movie *Mulan* it seemed that it would be Christina, not Britney, who would take the pop world by storm – especially when her début single 'Genie In A Bottle' got to Number 1 in the US and the UK in 1999.

It must have been galling for her, therefore, to see Britney racking up award after award, headline after headline, even though her own sales were far from unhealthy. It was perhaps because of this that Christina felt it necessary to push the boundaries of good clean fun to their limit with her raunchy stage act, in which she often appeared in leather chaps with only her skimpy knickers underneath and the word 'Nasty' scrawled across her backside. It certainly had the effect of upsetting the sensibilities of some parents, who complained to the British TV watchdog, the Independent Television Commission (ITC),

Atomic Kitten

It is hard to be unloved. In the late 1990s, Andy McCluskey must have looked in his shaving mirror every morning and wondered what exactly he'd done. After all, in the early 1980s his band OMD, formed in Liverpool with his buddy Paul Humphries, had been top of the world as their soaring hit 'Enola Gay' nuked the charts. But in an industry where 18 months is a lifetime, 20 years is eternity. Now the hits had dried. Humphries had left him and, despite his best efforts, the public could not get enthused about one Orchestral Manoeuvre in the Dark.

To cheer himself up, McCluskey decided he'd try his hand at the latest craze: creating and managing a bubblegum pop act. But, instead of a boy band, he decided on a female double act. Auditions were held in his home town and pretty soon McCluskey had his duo, Kerry Katona and Liz McLarnon, and a name, Automatic Kittens. McCluskey must have had mixed feelings as he signed them up and realised that neither had been born when 'Enola Gay' was at Number 1.

But something wasn't quite right. Natasha Hamilton was added to the mix and the name was shortened to Atomic Kitten and, as the new trio embarked on a series of showcase gigs in nightclubs in Liverpool and London, McCluskey realised that he might have a hit on his hands.

After signing to Innocent Records in August 1999, the girls were dispatched on the well-trodden route of school performances, Japanese gigs and supporting an already established teen group (in this case, 911). With McCluskey writing the songs and the Kittens wowing the teen audiences with their energy if not their singing, a hit was inevitable and arrived with the Top 10 single 'Right Now'.

When Katona started dating Westlife beefcake Bryan McFadden, the profile of the group was raised even further, as speculation grew feverish about British bubblegum's first wedding. In the end, fans had to settle for the next best thing, as Katona left the band to have a baby and was replaced by Jenny Frost. Fears that the line-up change would have a deleterious effect on the band were dismissed when the single 'Whole Again' topped the charts.

For McCluskey it was vindication, proof that he could still cut the mustard, for the Kittens, a claw mark in bubblegum history.

about one Saturday-morning kids' show which showed a graphic Aguilera video over the cornflakes. Dismissing the complaints, the ITC ruled: 'Undoubtedly some performers and music videos are more suggestive than in the past, reflecting considerable changes in society with regard to sexual behaviour as well pop music's inherent "boundary pushing" nature. There will always be some performers who deliberately court controversy for one reason or another.'

Quite what Walt Disney would have made of his fresh-faced Mouseketeers thrusting their groins into the camera lens is another matter, but the success of Spears, Timberlake, Aguilera and a subsequent rash of popsters including Nikki Deloach, Jennifer McGill, Terra McNair, Jason Minor and Tony Lucca proves that, even if you're over 70 with big ears, you can still be a major player in the world of bubblegum pop.

Popstarsacademyrivalsidol: Bubblegum On TV

Atomic Kitten, Boyzone, Destiny's Child, Westlife, Blue, 911, B*Witched, A1, 5ive, Steps, S Club 7, The Backstreet Boys, Tatu, Britney, Christina, Billie,

911: blueprint boy-band fodder for the under-eights

Honeyz, 'N Sync, Sugababes, M2M, Mis-teeq, Busted, Big Brovaz, Sammie, Jessica Simpson, A*Team, 98 Degrees…the dawn of the new millennium revealed a world literally infested with manufactured pop acts. The tentative creation of pop's pioneers had, nearly 50 years later, mutated into a fully blown Frankenstein's monster, its six-pack exposed, its hair and teeth bleached, and its skull empty. All the monster knew was that it was ravenous, that it had to feed its insatiable desire for bubblegum by consuming more and more raw material, and as it strode the world it found rich pastures of sustenance, fields of teenage wannabes swaying to the same sampled beat, pleading to be harvested.

But now, in the dawn of the millennium, the monster found that it no longer had to do the harvesting. There were TV programmes that would do it to order. The programmes were called *Popstars*, *Pop Idol*, *Popstars: The Rivals* and *Fame Academy*.

It seems incredible that with pop charts around the world groaning at the seams with manufactured bands, TV execs should choose to come up with a show designed to manufacture yet more. Yet they did. And not just one programme. Between 2001 and the end of 2002 there were no fewer than four such shows being screened in the UK alone, while the rights had been sold globally to countries as diverse as Argentina, South Africa, Australia, Denmark, Brazil, Germany, Japan and Singapore.

Popstars

Popstars began in Australia, where it proved an instant success and launched a girl group called Bardot to the top of their native charts. The format was simple: an advert was put in a trade paper asking for anyone who thought they had what it took to be a pop star to attend auditions. Then a selection of industry figures whittled down the thousands of hopefuls to a manageable number, before putting the rest through their paces over the course of several televised weeks. To add the necessary human interest, the remaining wannabes would be told to their faces whether they were either in or out. The five survivors would then be handed over to a top promoter, release a single and, hopefully, enjoy a modicum of success before returning to the oblivion from which they came.

In the UK, the project was masterminded by Nigel Lythgoe, a TV producer whose CV included that other Anglo-American smash, *Gladiators*. Lythgoe, who would later become known as 'Nasty Nigel' because of his abrasive style, roped in Paul Adam, A&R director at Polydor, and Nicki Chapman, former Spice Girls publicist, as his fellow judges and the three set about hacking their way through more than 20,000 hopefuls at six auditions around the UK. 'There is no formula for becoming a pop star,' Lythgoe said. 'It's all to do with a magical, indefinable ingredient called stardust.'

It was also all to do with ratings. As the wheat was separated from the chaff, *Popstars* was attracting huge Saturday-evening ratings. They were to get even bigger as the 33 survivors were slowly picked off like stragglers in the gun-sights of a sniper.

The five that were eventually chosen were: Noel Sullivan, 20, a waiter from Cardiff; Danny Foster, 21, a part-time cleaner from London; dancers Kym Marsh, 24, and Suzanne Shaw, 19, from Lancashire; and Myleene Klass, a former backing singer for Cliff Richard.

While *Popstars* gained ratings on the basis of the audience's grim fascination with seeing who was going to be kicked off next, it was of equal interest for the impartial observer, to see the lid lifted on the actual mechanics of producing and marketing a bubblegum band.

Within minutes of the band and its name, Hear'Say, being chosen, Granada TV's licensing department was feverishly cooking up ideas for marketing them. Discussions began for a package of merchandising, ranging from Hear'Say pyjamas and T-shirts, to cosmetics, CD-ROMs, a board game and dolls, although the fact that the group's identity was unknown right until the last minute made life difficult.

'We were having to market the group before we'd even finalised who would be in the group,' said Granada's licensing manager Sarah Christmas. 'There was a certain element of having to second-guess what their target audience would be interested in. Ultimately, we looked at the Spice Girls and how they became five separate entities.'

Following the well-trodden path was the name of the game as far as Hear'Say's sound and look was concerned. The group were put in the capable hands of songwriter Ray Hedges, who wrote Number 1 hits for Boyzone and B*Witched; they were produced by the team that produced 5ive, Honeyz and the Spice Girls; and their image consultant was Juice, the stylist responsible for the look of 5ive, Steps, A1 and S Club 7.

The song, 'Pure And Simple', and their hastily recorded eponymous album leaped straight to the top of the charts within 15 weeks of the group's inception – the fastest-selling British début of all time, and manufacturing at its purest and simplest.

It was not an approach that pleased everyone in the industry. 'It's unfortunate that music has become so disposable,' said Ed Bicknell, manager of Dire Straits. 'It can take a band three or four years of living in a van before they break a record. Hear'Say have managed all that in weeks.'

Other observers recognised the footprints of a previous era. '*Popstars* owes an overwhelming debt to Motown,' said pop author Craig Werner. 'This highly televised way of creating a pop group, then marketing their images via toys and other collectables, is exactly what Motown excelled at. And it pretty much set the standard for the way the pop industry – particularly with boy groups and girl groups – acquits itself today. *Popstars* is a repetition of all that, only with more speed.'

For a second generation of MTV viewers, *Popstars* was ideal fodder. The formula went around the world with the same success.

In the US, the three judges – choreographer Travis Payne, manager Jennifer Greig-Costin and record exec Jaymes Foster-Levy – whittled thousands of applicants down to just five girls, who became known as

Tatu's raunchy videos sparked controversy throughout the media but, ultimately, that was all they had to offer

Tatu

Tatu were bound to happen somewhere along the line: it was just a question of which Svengali would have the courage to take teen sex to the limit.

In the end, it wasn't Pete Waterman or Simon Fuller or Maurice Starr or Jeff Fenster. The man who created bubblegum pop's first lesbo lovers was a Russian psychologist, scriptwriter and director called Ivan Shapovalov who, sitting in his Moscow office one day in 2002, reasoned, 'Why the hell not?'

After auditioning 500 hopefuls, Shapovalov chose 16-year-old Lena Katina and Yulia Volkova, 15, to carry the hopes of the former Soviet Union into the pop charts of the capitalist West, with a routine that made Christina Aguilera look like a nun.

The omens were on his side. Their Russian début single, 'I've Lost My Mind', a tale of young lesbian love, had been a massive hit, especially with teenagers, and spawned the follow-ups 'Gayboy' (including the sensational lyric 'Gayboy, Gayboy. Be more cheeky with me') and 'They Won't Catch Us', complete with video in which an innocent airport worker is crushed by the duo's truck in a bid to let true love run its course.

In the video for their UK début single 'All The Things She Said', the girls, wearing skimpy school uniforms, were seen kissing and cuddling in a rainstorm. TV channels across the world queued up to ban the video, thus achieving instant global notoriety and a smash hit for Tatu. Meanwhile, Shapovalov fanned the flames by claiming, 'I got the idea from watching pornography on the Internet. Lena and Yulia are an underage sex project.'

They were also very much a one-trick pony. Selected as Russia's entry in the 2003 Eurovision Song Contest, they were expected to win by a street. Indeed organisers of the contest in Latvia had the recorded dress rehearsal on standby in case the girls got too carried away with each other during their live performance. In the end, Lena and Yulia simply looked bored with the whole thing, suggesting that they were as unconvinced by the red-hot lesbo act as everybody else.

– being willing to put up with humiliation, with incredible personal criticism and still stand your own ground.'

It was nothing of the sort, of course. *Pop Idol* was about kids wanting to be pop stars, to be as famous and rich as Ronan and Justin and Britney and Christina. They took part, not to stand their ground in the face of humiliation, but to show to the world that they had what Nigel Lythgoe described as '…that magical, indefinable ingredient called stardust'.

Popstars: The Rivals

The best thing about this interminable spin-off of *Popstars* was the verbal spat between bubblegum gurus Pete Waterman and Louis Walsh when it became clear that both were onto a loser. It was totally contrived, as one would expect of two of pop's premier hype-meisters, but it was a lot more entertaining than the no-hope bands who won the actual contest.

The idea of the show was similar to *Popstars*, except that at the end we would be left with a girl band and a boy band who would then fight it out for the 2002 Christmas Number 1. It would also be a contest of sorts between Walsh and Waterman, who would manage and promote the girl band and the boy band respectively.

There were two major flaws with the show, however. One was that, after *Popstars* and *Pop Idol*, the viewing public was heartily sick of the whole concept. The prospect of voting yet another bunch of nobodies into the charts had begun to pall. This was compounded by the second flaw, which was that the series went on for ever. Or maybe it just seemed that way.

Things only got interesting once the two groups had finally been chosen. Waterman immediately began talking up the boy band, One True Voice, by saying he was 'ecstatic' at the chance to manage them. 'In 40 years in the music business, I have not worked with any stars better than the boys,' he said.

Will Young: admitted he was gay and became even more popular with his teeny fans

His words also issued from the mouth of singer Keith, when he described their rivals Girls Aloud as having 'no talent. The girls can't sing live. They can't harmonise. When they tried to record their single they were so bad they ended up miming.'

Walsh, meanwhile, was having just as much fun. When Waterman claimed he would commit suicide if Girls Aloud got to Number 1, the Irishman said, 'Why not do it on live TV? That would be really great entertainment!'

It was all good, knockabout stuff but both gurus knew they were merely deflecting attention from the fact that One True Voice and Girls Aloud was jerry-built pop without a single decent foundation to support it. The girls got to Number 1 and the boys to Number 2, but that was a foregone conclusion. With singles sales plummeting, only a fraction of those who bothered to watch the show needed to buy the respective records to send them to the top. A more accurate indication of their popularity came when a nationwide tour featuring both bands was cancelled due to poor ticket sales. Behind the scenes,

Girls Aloud were created thanks to
Popstars: The Rivals – *but did anybody*
really care?

Waterman and Walsh would no doubt have shaken hands, gone for a slap-up meal and paid for it with the money they had earned from the exercise. For the two bands, only oblivion beckoned.

There was one more vaguely interesting sideshow to the Rivals, and that came in the shape of The Cheeky Girls, two statuesque twins from eastern Europe who had been rejected at an early stage in the auditions procedure but went on to reach the Top 10 with a piece of fluff called 'Cheeky Girls (Touch My Bum)'. Needless to say, they were never seen again.

Despite Pete Waterman, the bottom of the barrel was finally reached with One True Voice

Fame Academy

The fourth of a never-ending procession of create-a-star TV shows screened during 2002 was probably the most worthy, but for that reason it flopped disastrously in the ratings compared to the *Popstar/Pop Idol* franchises.

In this, a group of youngsters were dispatched to a country house, where they were drilled in the performing arts by a succession of stars (Lionel Ritchie, Shania Twain) and at the end of their time a winner was selected by a panel of judges. The winner was a sensitive young man called David Sneddon, who had utterly nothing going for him apart from the fact he was a hugely talented songwriter.

He probably still is.

Blue

It was difficult to tell exactly what Elton John was thinking as he sat like a benevolent uncle at his piano watching boy band Blue murder his 1970s classic, 'Sorry Seems To Be The Hardest Word'.
'You're not getting any younger, Elt – the money might come in handy'?
'Think of all the kudos, Elt – these kids are the biggest bubblegum band in Britain'?
Or was that faraway look in his eye because he was thinking about the days when young musicians like himself actually wrote songs instead of ripping them off.

Blue – alias Dunc, Ant, Lee and Simon – were the inevitable consequence of the auditions merry-go-round instigated by the likes of Simon Fuller. Recognising each other from the various queues they had fruitlessly stood in together over the years, they decided to cut out the middleman and form their own group.

'We just used to meet up at the house and practise a cappella harmonies and stuff,' Dunc revealed. 'It was a hobby at first, but then we got a manager and he got us signed up.'
The record label was Innocent, who also had Atomic Kitten [see ATOMIC KITTEN] on their books and were eagerly hoovering up any boy or girl band sent their way. The resulting single, 'Fly By II', was an immediate hit and Blue were off on the treadmill.

Searching for a ballad to consolidate their chart success in 2003, they decided to go for Elton John's 1976 masterpiece. Elton, smarting after the relative failure of his last album, *Songs From The West Coast*, agreed to perform with them, ostensibly to show that he was still in touch with modern trends. However, his powerful vocal performance noticeably dwarfed Blue's weedy warblings and served to make the point that there's talent and there's hype and there are few shades in between.

★

In the time it has taken you to read this book, another three boy bands will have been created somewhere in the world. They will have different names, different looks, different nationalities – but they will be exactly the same. They will be no older than 22, good-looking, worked-out, fit, keen and, most important of all, willing to do anything to be rich and famous. They will have a manager, probably in his late 20s or early 30s, who will be on a deal of not less than 25 per cent of their earnings. The manager will have already decided the characteristics of each member of the band; he will know who is the quiet, sensitive one, the one who likes to party, the one who is sports-mad. He will have ensured that the band members know this as well, just in case they are asked.

They will have already recorded a demo tape – reworked versions of 'Disco Inferno' by The Trammps and 'Too Much Heaven' by The Bee Gees, perhaps. Between them they will have worked out a ten-minute act for those nightclub bookings the manager is working on, some easily choreographed moves and basic close harmony. Hopefully they can get a radio slot. Maybe a piece on the local news. And who knows – maybe some record-company talent-spotter will see them, sign them up and send them on their way to the big time…

It's so simple, it's amazing that everyone isn't in a boy or a girl band. Mind you, as we approach the midway point in the first decade of the new millennium, almost 50 years from the day that manufactured pop was born (or should that be created), it seems that everyone under the age of 22 either is, or once was, or wants to be.

But this is not a modern phenomenon. If there is one thing to be learned from this trawl through half a century of plastic pop, it is that, while the faces may change, the rules remain the same.

1. There will always be a naive hopeful, there will always be a street-sharp Svengali to mould him, her or them into a marketable product: Fabian and Marucci/DeAngelis; Tommy Hicks and Larry Parnes; Priscilla White and Brian Epstein; The Saxons and Tam Paton; The New Kids and Maurice Starr; John Lydon and Malcolm McLaren; Rick Astley and Pete Waterman; Geri, Victoria, the two Mels and Emma and Simon Fuller.

2. There will always be an audience to buy their records, to scream at them, to buy their merchandise and plead undying love to them.

3. They will be at the top for two years maximum.

4. They will be fond memories in five years, forgotten in ten.

This is why, when people question whether manufactured pop is valid, the answer must always be a resounding 'Yes!' OK, the music is mostly uninspired and the acts more often than not vacuous puppets, but bubblegum is not designed for any permanency. It is not high art. It exists only for the moment in which it is created. And if we all had the skill to exploit that moment like Pete Waterman, if we could all write songs like Jerry Kasenetz and Jeff Katz, and if we could all sing them like Donny Osmond, then we'd all be as rich as they are.

THE BEST OF THE WORST?
THE TOP 20 BUBBLEGUM HITS OF ALL TIME

Is it possible to sum-up plastic pop? Probably not, so diverse have been the methods and ingredients used to create manufactured artists over the last 50 years. But if they ever released an album called *Now That's What I Call Bubblegum*, the following hits would undoubtedly be vying for inclusion.

1. THE ARCHIES: 'Sugar Sugar' (1969)
Classic manufactured pop right down to its animated toes.

2. THE VILLAGE PEOPLE: 'YMCA' (1978)
Everyone knows the moves for this designer-gay disco belter.

3. JASON DONOVAN AND KYLIE MINOGUE: 'Especially For You' (1988)
The inevitable cheesy duet by the dream duo hyped by Hit Man Pete Waterman.

4. MILLI VANILLI: 'Girl You Know It's True' (1988)
Chart-topper by the band who never sang on their records.

5. FRANKIE GOES TO HOLLYWOOD: 'Relax' (1984)
Lavish production and oodles of hype – a blueprint for plastic popsters.

6. FRANKIE LYMON AND THE TEENAGERS: 'I'm Not A Juvenile Delinquent' (1957)
The first black boy band were marketed as white, in contrast to modern white boys who pretend they're from the 'hood.

7. THE MONKEES: 'I'm A Believer' (1967)
Created for TV, the Monkees also had the advantage of some of the finest songwriters of their generation. This was just one classic track.

8. DONNY OSMOND: 'Puppy Love' (1972)
Pure schmaltz from the era when Osmondmania swept the globe.

9. THE BAY CITY ROLLERS: 'Bye Bye Baby' (1975)
The song which launched tartan teen hysteria.

10. THE SEX PISTOLS: 'Anarchy In The UK' (1977)
Created national outrage – which was just what Malcolm McLaren wanted.

11. NEW EDITION: 'Candy Girl' (1983)
The Jackson 5 clones created by Maurice Starr enjoyed a huge hit with this one before turning into hiphop-sters.

12. NEW KIDS ON THE BLOCK: 'Hangin' Tough' (1990)
These middle-class white boys pinched the hiphop vibe from the ghetto and became megastars.

13. WILL YOUNG AND GARETH GATES: 'Unchained Melody' (2001)
Phone-vote winner and loser joined forces to prove that there were no hard feelings.

14. BOYZONE: 'Love Me For A Reason' (1994)
Just one of many insipid cover versions churned out by the Irish boy band.

15. TOMMY STEELE: 'Rock With The Caveman' (1957)
Hard to believe that this record turned cheeky Cockney Tommy Steele into Britain's first official rock 'n' roll star.

16. RACEY: 'Some Girls' (1979)
One of Chinn and Chapman's school of session musician stars.

17. ONE TRUE VOICE: 'Sacred Trust' (2003)
The moment when plastic pop finally scraped the bottom of the barrel.

18. SIGUE SIGUE SPUTNIK: 'Love Missile F1-11' (1986)
Cynical self-publicists, yet they still managed to fool the record-buying public.

19. TIFFANY: 'I Think We're Alone Now' (1988)
Atonal squawking from the queen of the shopping malls.

20. BLUE FEATURING ELTON JOHN: 'Sorry Seems To Be The Hardest Word' (2003)
As the boy band murdered one of his finest songs, Elton gamely played on and counted the royalties.

SELECT BIBLIOGRAPHY

Baker, Glenn A, *et al*, *Monkees: Monkeemania*, Plexus 1999

Barlow, Gary, *Take That: The Greatest Book Ever*, Virgin 1996

Boy George (with Spencer Bright), *Take It Like A Man*, Pan 1995

Daley, Marsha, *The Osmonds – A Family Biography*, St Martin's, 1983

Dannen, Frederick, *Hit Men: Power Brokers And Fast Money Inside The Music Business*, Muller, 1990

Gibbs, Alvin, Destroy, *The Definitive History Of Punk*, Britannia Press, 1996

Glitter, Gary, *Leader: The Autobiography Of Gary Glitter*, Ebury Press, 1991

Guralnick, Peter, *Last Train To Memphis: The Rise Of Elvis Presley*, Abacus, 1995

Hylton, Stuart, *From Rationing To Rock: The 1950s Revisited*, Sutton, 1998

Kennedy, John, *Tommy Steele: The Facts About A Teenage Idol And An Inside Picture of Showbusiness*, Burns, 1958

Larkin, Colin (editor), *The Virgin Encyclopedia of Popular Music*, Virgin, 2002

Malone, Maria, *Popstars, The Making Of Hear'Say*, Granada, 2001

Napier-Bell, Simon, *Black Vinyl, White Powder*, Ebury, 2001

Posner, Gerald L, *Motown: Money, Power, Sex And Music*, Random House, 2002

Smith, Giles, Lost In Music, Picador, 1995

Wale, Michael, *The Bay City Rollers*, Everest, 1975

INDEX

Page numbers in *italics* refer to illustrations and those in **bold** to main entries